# The Best News Possible: You May Live Forever!

George T. Javor

**TEACH Services, Inc.**
PUBLISHING
www.TEACHServices.com • (800) 367-1844

All rights reserved. No part of this publication may be reproduced, distributed, or transmitted in any form or by any means, including photocopying, recording, or other electronic or mechanical methods, without the prior written permission of the publisher, except in the case of brief quotations embodied in critical reviews and certain other noncommercial uses permitted by copyright law. For permission requests, write to the publisher, TEACH Services, Inc., at the address below.

Copyright © 2020 George T. Javor
Copyright © 2020 TEACH Services, Inc.
ISBN-13: 978-1-4796-1244-4 (Paperback)
ISBN-13: 978-1-4796-1245-1 (ePub)
Library of Congress Control Number: 2020912683

All Scripture quotations, unless otherwise indicated, are taken from the New Living Translation, Copyright © 1996, 2004, 2015 by Tyndale House Foundation. Used by permission.

Scripture quotations marked NKJV are taken from the New King James Version®. Copyright © 1990 by Thomas Nelson. Used by permission. All rights reserved.

Scripture quotations marked KJV are taken from the King James Version® of the Bible. Public domain.

Scripture quotations marked NIV are taken from the New International Version, Copyright © 1973, 1978, 1984, 2011 by Biblica, Inc.® Used by permission. All rights reserved worldwide.

Scripture quotations marked BSB are taken from The Holy Bible, Berean Study Bible. Copyright © 2016, 2018 by Bible Hub. Used by Permission. All Rights Reserved Worldwide.

The website references in this book have been shortened using a URL shortener and redirect service called 1ref.us, which TEACH Services manages. If you find that a reference no longer works, please contact us and let us know which one is not working so that we can correct it. Any personal website addresses that the author included are managed by the author. TEACH Services is not responsible for the accuracy or permanency of any links.

Published by

www.TEACHServices.com • (800) 367-1844

# Dedication

This book is dedicated first to Shirley, my wife and soul mate. And second, to kindred souls everywhere, who occasionally take time to contemplate the miracle of existence.

# Table of Contents

Chapter 1: The Best News Possible! . . . . . . . . . . . . . . . . . . . . . . . . . . . 5

Chapter 2: A Library Out of This World . . . . . . . . . . . . . . . . . . . . . . . . 9

Chapter 3: A Recurring Nightmare. . . . . . . . . . . . . . . . . . . . . . . . . . . 41

Chapter 4: The History of Tomorrow . . . . . . . . . . . . . . . . . . . . . . . . . 49

Chapter 5: Eternal Bliss . . . . . . . . . . . . . . . . . . . . . . . . . . . . . . . . . . . 65

*Appendix 1: How Radioactivity is Used to Estimate the*
    *Age of the Earth*. . . . . . . . . . . . . . . . . . . . . . . . . . . . . . . . . . . . . 80

*Appendix 2: Biblical Data on the Age of the Earth* . . . . . . . . . . . . . . . 82

*Appendix 3: The Golden Phone*. . . . . . . . . . . . . . . . . . . . . . . . . . . . . 83

*Bibliography* . . . . . . . . . . . . . . . . . . . . . . . . . . . . . . . . . . . . . . . . . . . 89

## Chapter 1

# The Best News Possible!

An elderly, well-to-do gentleman heard from his wife, "Dear, you better start spending some of your money because you can't take it with you where you're going." "If I can't take it with me," replied the hubby, "I am not going!"

Aside from the unexpected answer, don't we all share the oldster's sentiment? The real absurdity is that we all have to go sooner or later, against our will! None of us want to part with family, friends, possessions—ever. There is no substitute to being alive! Unless we battle a painful terminal illness, we long to continue on. As long as there is life, there are always prospects for improvement, if not miracles!

Though we know that life inevitably ends, we don't dwell on it. Thinking about death is a morbid downer. It spoils our finest moments, robs us of joy and tranquility. Who wants to deal with the shocking reality that all humanity is on death row?

If you ask elderly readers of newspapers why they go to the obituary notices first, they tell you that they are checking to see if one of their friends passed away. They also note the ages of the deceased to see how they stack up against them in longevity.

This interest in life span comes to us gradually after the age of fifty because at birthday time, almost subconsciously, we multiply our years by two, and until we are fifty we come up with a fairly reasonable, "attainable" number. So what if we end up in the seventies, eighties or nineties? "Many people reach those years," we reason. We are satisfied that we have a long, expected life span ahead of us and we set aside this topic until our next birthday.

But at age fifty, things change. Now, if we dare to multiply our years by two, we come up with unacceptable numbers and ages that are likely out of our reach. Thus, after fifty we stop this game and we try to come to terms with our aging selves.

The admonition: "Don't worry about old age, it does not last long" is, unfortunately, true. Time begins to speed up in the second half of our lives and the more we fight to slow it down, the faster it goes!

Regardless of how successful and contented we are, the problem of aging is the 800-pound gorilla that follows us everywhere. Would it not be radical, and completely beyond fantastic, if there were a way out from our short life span prison? We are talking about living for hundreds, thousands, millions of years, or for that matter, forever! But not in a world such as we have today. It would be torture to witness the daily horrors we now see around us. Many of the stories that fill the daily news turn our stomachs, rob us of tranquility and force us to disengage from following too closely what goes on in the world.

*Is it too much to wish for living in a society filled with goodness and love in perpetuity? The best new possible is that this is not a wishful fantasy! We are talking about the fulfillment of the original intent of our Maker!*

Is it too much to wish for living in a society filled with goodness and love in perpetuity? The best new possible is that this is not a wishful fantasy! We are talking about the fulfillment of the original intent of our Maker!

Where does the desire to live forever come from? It has been noted that we all live with fundamental, non-negotiable biological needs: hunger, thirst, sensitivity to extreme cold or heat and the need for companionship. It is remarkable that there are perfectly satisfying means of alleviating all of them.

Frustrating as it may be, however, we cannot take care of this most fundamental and deepest of needs: to live in perpetuity. Here we run up against a brick wall, the apparent absence of means to accomplish it. The will to live is not unique to us; every organism, from bacteria to mankind has it, but only humans are conscious of their finite life span.

Our instinct leads us to the writings and pronouncements of the wisest and most accomplished men and women of our times. Included are the scientists who have uncovered many of the mysteries of the physical world, philosophers who have spent their lives contemplating existence, artists and musicians who have blessed us with their talents and insights. But alas, they have nothing that can help us.

Our thought leaders teach that our existence and everything around us is the result of a myriad of fortuitous events. Starting with an enormous explosion, the Big Bang, a gigantic and complex universe came into existence. It is not exactly clear just what exploded since there was nothing in the universe before it. However murky the picture, the explosion is stipulated because the narrative cannot proceed without it. Over billions of years, stars and planets emerged and coalesced into galaxies and solar systems by the billions. Life sprung up on earth because conditions were favorable in every conceivable way.

The overarching philosophy driving leading contemporary thinkers is that physical matter is the only reality there is and that all beings, processes and phenomena can be explained as manifestations of matter.

In the future, scientists will find out more and more about the structure of matter as subatomic particles are smashed into smithereens in gigantic particle accelerators. They plan to explain the nature of gravitation and the forces now known only as positive and negative charges. We will learn more and more about the history of earth after scientists explore the solar system more completely. Astronomers will continue to monitor outer space for intelligent signals. Biologists will soon show how life could have started on earth and proliferated into millions of distinct species.

Although we may not live long enough to get final and complete answers that explain what we are doing here and why, it is certain that answers will be found sometime in the future, satisfying all our curiosities.

This optimism fuels the continued funding of research related to origins. Current trends actually appear to go in the opposite direction: the more we drill into the puzzle of existence, the more mysterious and unsolvable it becomes. But the night is the darkest just before dawn.

Though materialism is an impressive doctrine, it does not satisfy our deepest yearnings. Perhaps they cannot be satisfied! Modern science and philosophy push us toward accepting our status quo as the best we can hope for. Existence, as far as can be determined, has no deep meaning or significance other than its obvious but temporary charms. The take-home lesson is crystal clear: *Carpe Diem!* (Seize the day!) Live fully every minute because you do not have a guarantee of the next minute, never mind tomorrow!

To be sure, there exists an ancient collection of writings from a primitive, prescientific age written by people who knew nothing of biology, chemistry, physics or quantum mechanics. Thought leaders of our day summarily dismiss these documents as primitive, absurd and thoroughly discredited by modern science.[1] They do not waste their precious time considering their content and suggest that we follow their example.

These ancient writings present a concept so preposterous, insulting to the intelligence of a rational, twenty-first century's educated person, that one hesitates even to articulate it. They state that mankind did not evolve from primitive organisms, but was actually created to live in perpetuity! Interestingly, this resonates with our deeply embedded expectation for eternal existence which many dare not even contemplate for fear of ridicule. Could these be echoes within us of the biblical story of Creation?

The following chapters are journeys into this now-abandoned territory, free of twenty-first century prejudices, away from the disapproving frowns of contemporary wise persons. It is more fantastic than James Hilton's *Shangri-La*[2] and it is here we discover the secret of eternal and completely happy existence!

---

[1]L.R. Godfrey, Scientists Confront Creationists (Toronto: George J. McLeod Limited, 1983), p. 324 & T.M. Berra, Evolution and the Myth of Creationism (Stanford, CA: Standford University Press, 1990), p. 198.
[2]James Hilton, The Lost Horizon (New York, NY: William Morrow and Co, 1933).

## Chapter 2

# A Library Out of This World

An emaciated, poorly dressed man came to see the minister. "I am down on my luck," he explained, "I am at the end of my rope. Can you help me?" The pastor looked the man in the eye. "The answer you are seeking is right in here," he said and handed him a Bible.

Four weeks later the man returned. This time he was dressed to a T. His eyes beamed with joy as he said to the pastor, "I cannot thank you enough for your help! Things are really looking up for me!" "I am glad that you are doing so well. How did the Bible help you turn things around?" "Well," said the man, "I took the Bible you gave me, closed my eyes and opened it randomly. What do you suppose I saw when I opened my eyes?" The minister's curiosity was palpable. "CHAPTER ELEVEN!"

This use of the Good Book is not advocated here. The Bible, a library of sixty-six books written over a period of approximately 1,500 years, does not contain magic formulas. But some of its content is literally out of this world! We are talking about extraterrestrial information! How else can we explain the Bible describing the very origin of everything on the globe from the perspective of an eyewitness?

The Bible also records communications between select persons and non-human messengers (angels). Prophets wrote the contents of their visions and dreams. The messages often came at critical times in history.

The book of Daniel contains a remarkable prophecy that describes the world's history until its very end. This revelation will be discussed in the chapter, "The History of Tomorrow."

> *Communications from above did not stop in the first century AD. Over the past 2,000 years the Holy Spirit has prompted many faithful men and women to bless humanity with their writings.*

Communications from above did not stop in the first century AD. Over the past 2,000 years the Holy Spirit has prompted many faithful men and women to bless humanity with their writings. One such person was Ellen G. White (1827–1915). Along with her husband James White, and Joseph Bates, she is credited with founding the Seventh-day Adventist protestant denomination. During her lifetime she wrote more than 5,000 periodical articles and forty books.[3] Many of these are widely available for anyone to read and judge their contents for their value.

\*\*\*

The secular world at large, which has already rejected biblical content as of no serious value, is doing its very best to reach out to the great unknown in the cosmos. Extensive search for life on other planets of the solar system has revealed that life is present only here on earth. But there is a strong general consensus among today's thought leaders that ours is not the only civilization in the universe. If life developed accidentally on earth over eons of time, why should this not happen as well on some of the millions of planets in our Milky Way Galaxy? If there are other living beings out there, perhaps they are more advanced than we are! It would be superb to receive affirmation of the secular view of the universe, that we are but one of many independently evolved civilizations seeking to link up with other beings in the galaxy!

---

[3] "Ellen G. White," Wikipedia, https://1ref.us/17q (accessed 5/5/2020).

# A Library Out of This World

The construction of the world's largest single-aperture radio-telescope, located in China's Guizhou Province, was completed in July 3, 2016 at a cost of $180 million. The diameter of the dish is 500 meters (1,650ft) and its surface could cover 30 football fields. Project officials state that the facility should be very useful detecting signals that may have originated in distant alien civilizations.

From the 1960s to the present, increasingly sophisticated SETI (Search for Extra-Terrestrial Intelligence) programs have been carried out using gigantic radio telescopes reaching out into space. These huge electronic ears, with single antennas up to 3,300 feet in diameter, constantly listen to and analyze radio signals bombarding earth on millions of channels.[4]

But the most powerful radio telescope is a combination of twenty-seven parabolic dishes, each eighty-two feet in diameter, near Sorocco, NM, on the plain San Augustine, called the Very Large Array Radio Telescope. Each dish can be moved independently by transporters along rails laid out in a Y pattern. Each arm of the Y extends thirteen miles. A computer integrates the radio signals collected by the dishes. The maximum resolving power of the array is equivalent to a single parabolic dish with a diameter of an unbelievable twenty-two miles![5]

These projects cost millions of dollars, but if contact with extraterrestrials could be established the consensus is that money was well spent! As of now (2020), there have been no such contacts. Apparently heaven is not communicating through radio waves!

Thus, on one hand important messages from space right there between the covers of the Bible are unappreciated or ignored. On the other hand, we spend millions of dollars on fruitless efforts to contact extraterrestrials.

Though overlooked by the leaders of society, the Bible is a storehouse of astounding material from the cosmos, yielding information about humanity's past, present and future. Deep questions concerning the purpose of existence, the place of our world in the universe and

> *Though overlooked by the leaders of society, the Bible is a storehouse of astounding material from the cosmos, yielding information about humanity's past, present and future. Deep questions concerning the purpose of existence, the place of our world in the universe and where we are in the stream of this world's history are answered.*

---

[4] "Search for extraterrestrial intelligence," Wikipedia, https://1ref.us/17r (accessed 5/5/2020); https://1ref.us/192 (accessed 5/27/2020).
[5] The Editors of Encyclopaedia Britannica, "Very Large Array," Encyclopaedia Britannica, https://1ref.us/17s (accessed 5/5/2020).

The Karl J. Jansky Very Large Array radio-telescope system, located on the plains of San Augustine, near Sorocco New Mexico. Astronomers, using this facility, have made key observations about black holes, traced complex gas motions at the center of the Milky Way Galaxy, and provided new knowledge about the physical mechanisms that produce radio emissions.

where we are in the stream of this world's history are answered. In contrast to the *Star Wars* series of movies, it is in the Bible that we discover the true moral fabric of the universe.

We are assured that we are certainly not alone in the universe! Nor are we ignored. From the very beginning of our existence, heaven has solicitously watched every step and misstep of mankind, continuously attempting to steer our affairs for our good. We learn that earth is the focal point of an ongoing cosmic war between the forces of good and evil. Though penned thousands of years ago, the usefulness of biblical information is timeless! Even more to the point, it is in the Bible that we find the exciting details of the best news possible, the "how" to obtain the right to live forever in a new world remade by the Creator!

\*\*\*

The content of the Bible may be placed into three broad categories: 1: Creation. 2: The Fall of Mankind. 3: The Redemption of Mankind. We will explore these concepts in the following pages.

\*\*\*

# Creation

The Bible begins with an account of the Creation of the earth, the solar system, earth's biosphere and the origin of humanity. The Creator named here in Hebrew is *Elohim*, the plural of the singular term, *Elohenu*, and translated as "God."

We learn that the Creator accomplished the Creation of earth in six twenty-four hour days, and He rested on the seventh day. This day was called the Sabbath. Mankind was enjoined to observe every seventh day from that point on by ceasing from ordinary work (Gen. 1:1; 2:2–3).

By this narrative the Bible answers two questions: 1: How is it that we divide time into weeks when there is no astronomical reason to do so? 2: How is it that the word "Sabbath," or a derivative of it, is the name of the seventh day of the week in more than 100 languages? The simplest explanation is that the biblical story of Creation was in the collective memory of mankind before the great divergence of humanity into many languages and races.

The Bible begins with this sentence: "In the beginning God created the heavens [literally, the skies] and the earth" (Gen. 1:1). Whatever information we have about the Originator of the world comes from the Bible. He cannot be compared to anyone we know. He commands us not to create any image of Him and to be very sparing in using His name. The most often used reference to Him is *Adonai* (the Lord) or *Adonai Elohanu* (the Lord God).

The first stunning concept about God is that He has always existed. God calls Himself the "I AM," the eternal, self-existing One (Exod. 3:14). He is the only Being without a beginning! Moses puts it this way: "Lord, thou hast been our dwelling place in all generations. Before the mountains were brought forth, or ever thou hadst formed the earth and the world, even from everlasting to everlasting, thou art God" (Ps. 90:1–2, KJV). As finite beings we do not have the capacity to grasp what infinity is, especially looking backwards. But there had to be a literally timeless period of immeasurable length with only God in existence.

The plural name of the Creator, *Elohim*, immediately suggests that there is more than one Person included in this name. In fact, the Bible identifies God as a family of three distinct Persons, the Father, the Son and the Holy Spirit (Matt. 28:19; 2 Cor. 13:14). The terms "Godhead" or "Trinity" are used to refer to Their combined activities.

Unquestionably, there always was and always will be complete love and harmony between the Members of the Trinity. No one knows what occurred during the timeless pre-Creation period. If Their aim was to enjoy the infinite bliss of love for Each Other, satisfying Each Other's needs, nothing more had to happen. There never would have been a universe.

The Godhead, however, after undoubtedly a great deal of deliberation and planning, decided to create stars, planets and galaxies by the billions. The extent and depth of the Godhead's deliberations may be best described by the statement attributed to God Himself: "For *as* the heavens are higher than the earth, so are My ways higher than your ways, and My thoughts than your thoughts" (Isa. 55:9, NKJV).

The entire universe is a finite construct, currently estimated to be a sphere with a diameter of 93 billion light years and containing perhaps 2 trillion galaxies![6]

Thus, the Lord, who does not have a beginning, in creating our solar system performed something He did trillions of times previously. Knowing nothing about other galaxies, we can still be confident that our

---

[6]"Universe," Wikipedia, https://1ref.us/17t (accessed 5/5/2020) & Henry Fountain, "Two Trillion Galaxies, at the Very Least," New York Times, October 17, 2016.

newly created solar system is unique in the universe. Just as there are no truly identical snowflakes, grains of sand, microorganisms or human beings (including identical twins!), our Maker is definitely not a cookie cutter Creator!

The Hebrew verb in the first sentence of the Bible: "In the beginning God created the heavens and the earth" (Gen. 1:1), is *bara*, translated as "created." Significantly, there is no English equivalent for this Hebrew word, as its subject is exclusively God! In Hebrew, only the Lord can *bara* (create), living or non-living entities ex nihilo.

The first law of thermodynamics states that the energy content of the universe is constant. Albert Einstein discovered the equivalence of matter and energy, $E = mc^2$.[7] Therefore, the first law may be rephrased, "The energy/matter content of the universe is constant." Still, when the Creator *bara* (creates) stars and planets, He violates this law. The Lord is not imprisoned within the universe. He can modify its energy/matter content at will!

> *A foundational biblical truth is that God preceded everything, therefore He is the Originator of everything in existence! It follows that nothing in existence is truly independent of the Creator!*

A foundational biblical truth is that God preceded everything, therefore He is the Originator of everything in existence! It follows that nothing in existence is truly independent of the Creator!

To appreciate the phenomenal accomplishment of bringing the earth and the solar system into existence, we ask, "How hard is it to make matter?" Can humans manufacture matter in the laboratory? The answer is, "Yes!" Our best accomplishment, thus far, was in September of 1997 when a beam of electrons, traveling at nearly the speed of light in the two-mile-long linear accelerator at Stanford University, collided with a four terawatt burst of laser of light beam. (Four terawatt of energy is approximately half the total amount of energy the entirety of the USA households use in one day.) As the electron beam bumped into a light particle (photon) and knocked it backwards into the oncoming stream of high-energy photons, an electron/positron pair was

---

[7]Howard DeVoe, Thermodynamics and Chemistry. Second Edition, online version 10, page 58.

The Stanford Linear Accelerator Center (now called the SLAC National Accelerator Laboratory), located in Menlo Park, California, is the site of the 2 mile long linear accelerator, which could boost electrons to 99.9999999 percent of the speed of light.

produced for a fleeting moment before matter (electron) and anti-matter (positron) annihilated each other.[8]

The smallest atom, hydrogen, consists of a proton and an electron. The electron's mass is only a tiny fraction $(1/1,800)^{th}$ of the atomic mass of the proton, $1.67 \times 10^{-27}$ kg (0.000000000000000000000000000167 kg).[9]

To create a proton in the laboratory, a procedure similar to electron production could be done using a laser beam that is 1,000 times more powerful. Current technologies (pun not intended) are inadequate for such a procedure.

Impressive as it is to create an electron for a fleeting moment in the laboratory, it is eye-opening to compare it with the permanent creation of the entire mass of earth during Creation week: $6 \times 10^{24}$ kg or $3.6 \times 10^{51}$ times the mass of a hydrogen atom! This number, multiplied by 1,800 is the ratio of the Creator's accomplishment to human efforts.

In reference to the Creation of earth, we read in the Bible, "For thus saith the LORD that created the heavens; God himself that formed the earth and made it; he hath established it, he created it not in vain, he formed it to be inhabited: I am the LORD; and there is none else" (Isa. 45:18, KJV). May we not take this statement to mean that the reason the Creator brought worlds into existence is to populate them with living beings? The Godhead wanted to share the joy of existence with His creatures!

Indeed, there may well exist unnumbered billions of planets in the universe where created beings, who are not human, live happily in perpetuity. Unfortunately, because we would like to know so much more about them, there is just a fleeting reference to them in the Bible:

> Where wast thou when I laid the foundations of the earth? declare, if thou hast understanding. Who hath laid the measures thereof, if thou knowest? or who hath stretched the line upon it? Whereupon are the foundations thereof fastened? or who laid the corner stone thereof; When the morning stars sang together, and all the sons of God shouted for joy? (Job 38:4–7, KJV)

The term "sons of God" refers to the first individuals created on a planet. We reach this conclusion from looking at the genealogy of Jesus in the book of Luke: "Kenan was the son of Enosh. Enosh was the son

---
[8] University Of Rochester, "Out Of Pure Light, Physicists Create Particles Of Matter," ScienceDaily, https://1ref.us/17u (accessed 5/5/2020).
[9] "Electron," Wikipedia, https://1ref.us/17v (accessed 5/5/2020).

of Seth. Seth was the son of Adam. Adam was the son of God" (Luke 3:38). The sons of God are representatives of the planets they inhabit. The Creation of earth took place in the full view of these representatives of the universe and they shouted with joy! Contrary to Hollywood, we live in a friendly universe. No one is trying to invade us, annihilate us or take our resources!

Ellen White describes the newly created earth, as it was shown to her:

> As the earth came forth from the hand of its Maker, it was exceedingly beautiful. Its surface was diversified with mountains, hills, and plains, interspersed with noble rivers and lovely lakes; but the hills and mountains were not abrupt and rugged, abounding in terrific steeps and frightful chasms, as they now do; the sharp, ragged edges of earth's rocky framework were buried beneath the fruitful soil, which everywhere produced a luxuriant growth of verdure. There were no loathsome swamps or barren deserts. Graceful shrubs and delicate flowers greeted the eye at every turn .... The entire landscape outvied in beauty the decorated grounds of the proudest palace.[10]

In contrast to today's geography, where oceans occupy two-thirds of the earth's surface, the newly created globe was largely habitable. A canopy of water, high in the atmosphere, dispersed the sunlight evenly. The sky was uniformly radiant blue and, unlike today, evenly lit. No one could be blinded looking up toward the heavens since sunlight did not come from a single direction. As a result, there were no shadows anywhere. The water canopy high in the atmosphere also refracted the sun's rays back toward space, and from there, earth appeared wrapped in a giant rainbow. There were no clouds in the sky. Vegetation was watered by a fine mist which rose from an elaborate network of water-carrying tunnels beneath the earth's surface (Gen. 2:5–6).

The biosphere, which includes all vegetation and every living entity, had to come into existence rapidly because no organism is capable of survival by itself. Plants depend on nitrogen-fixing microorganisms in their roots and on carbon dioxide exhaled by animals. Animals, in turn, require oxygen which is made by plants through photosynthesis. The basic theme of the biosphere is interdependence and mutual support among living things.

---

[10]Ellen G. White, Patriarchs and Prophets (Mountain View, CA: Pacific Press, 1890), p. 44.

Two types of organisms were created: 1: Sentient creatures, which have nervous systems, brains, memories and sense pain. All animals, fish, birds and insects belong to this class. 2: Non-sentient organisms, without nervous systems, such as vegetation, trees, bushes and microorganisms. This class of creatures, bio-robots, was designed to sustain the lives of sentient beings. All organisms were created to live on vegetables, grains, nuts and fruits. Predation did not exist.

The astounding abundance of living organisms in today's biosphere leads the indifferent sojourner to overlook their presence. Everywhere we look we find living organisms. There is not a place on earth where a gram of soil does not contain at least 10,000 bacterial cells. Invisible bacterial spores float in the air.

Anyone who wants to test this fact may leave a sheet of freshly sliced potato on the kitchen counter. In a few days, colonies of bacteria and mold will appear on the potato slices. This is why we see hospital personnel in surgical suites, covered from head to toe in pre-sterilized garb.

Since the middle of the twentieth century, a scientific revolution has been raging, centering on biology (literally "the study of life"). It displaced physics, which used to be the most important natural science. The progress in understanding biology is nothing short of breathtaking! Yet, in spite of all this concerted attention on everything that has to do with living organisms, scientists are still having a difficult time defining what "life" is. More importantly, they cannot produce even the simplest living entity. The emerging field of synthetic biology came into existence in the late twentieth century for the expressed goal to manufacture life in the laboratory. As of now, they have not reached their goal and in the opinion of this writer, they never will![11]

Regarding biology, one of the most frustrating conundrums of modern science is the origin of life on earth. Significantly, many of the founders of modern science were devout creationists holding, as creationists,

*The progress in understanding biology is nothing short of breathtaking! Yet, in spite of all this concerted attention on everything that has to do with living organisms, scientists are still having a difficult time defining what "life" is.*

---

[11]G. T. Javor, A Scientist Celebrates Creation (Ringold, GA: Teach Services Inc., 2012), pp. 14–15.

that life came to earth by divine fiat. This writer, in a letter to the editor of the Microbe magazine[12] (the monthly publication of the American Society for Microbiology), pointed out this fact in response to a warning by the National Academy of Sciences, USA, against "diluting science" by teaching creationism in the classroom.[13] Respondents to this letter did not dispute the crucially important contributions creation scientists played in establishing modern science. Rather, they claimed that if the founders of modern science were alive today, they all would be evolutionists. Perhaps so, but it escaped their notice that their scientific edifice rests on foundations built by creationists!

Current textbooks of biology and biochemistry, dealing with the topic of origins of life on earth, uniformly refer to the work of Stanley Miller as the beginning of a new field of discovery—chemical evolution. A graduate student in the laboratory of the Nobel Prize winner, Harold Urey, in 1953 published a ground-breaking paper in which he described the production of some amino acids in a device that contained the postulated gases of a primordial atmosphere on a primitive, lifeless earth. The circulating gases in the closed glass chambers were exposed to continuous electrical discharge for a week, simulating hypothetical events prior to the appearance of life.[14]

Since amino acids are the building blocks of the all-important substance, protein, here was the first laboratory demonstration of how life could have come into being on a primitive earth. Numerous laboratories

---

[12]G.T. Javor, Letters to Microbe Magazine, vol. 3, Number 5, 2008. For unknown reason, this particular volume is missing from the archives of *Microbe Magazine* of the American Society for Microbiology. For this reason, the letter is reproduced here:

> "Evolution in the Classroom" Risking the ire of the National Academy of Sciences, attention needs to be called to the irony in their current crusade against creationism in science classrooms. Sir Francis Bacon, who is credited with formulating and establishing the scientific method was a creationist. So were Sir Isaac Newton, Robert Boyle, Louis Pasteur, Carl Linnaus, Michael Faraday, Blaise Pascal, Lord Kelvin, James Clerk Maxwell, Jean Louis Agassiz, Rudolph Carl Virchow, Johannes Kepler and numerous other intellectual giants on whose shoulders stand the modern scientific enterprise. Clearly, creationism did not hinder the scientific work of these greats, rather it encouraged them to seek keener insights into the secrets of the physical realm. Permitting students to peek outside the box of evolution is hardly a dilution of science. Rather it is granting them freedom of imagination and thought similar to what students of previous generations were allowed to have."
> 
> George T. Javor, Loma Linda University School of Medicine
> Loma Linda, California

[13]National Academy of Sciences, Science and Creationism: A View from the National Academy of Sciences, 2nd ed. (Washington, DC: The National Academies Press, 1999), https://1ref.us/193 (accessed 5/27/2020).

[14]S. L. Miller, "Production of amino acids under primitive earth conditions," Science, May 15, 1953, pp. 528–529.

quickly joined the search for creating biologically relevant substances from proposed primordial gases and the discipline of "chemical evolution" was born. As more and more biologically relevant substances were produced under a variety of postulated primordial conditions, chemical evolutionary scientists became increasingly optimistic of explaining how life could have developed on earth. A perfect opportunity to show the validity of their theories came in the 1970s when the U.S. space program was ready to explore the planet Mars.

Among earth's neighbors in the solar system, Mars is considered to be the most hospitable to life as we know it. The surface temperature of Mars never rises above 86 °F, and the average surface temperature of Mars is only 122 °F colder than earth. Conditions on the surface of Mars are certainly less hostile than those of the boiling hot springs of Yellowstone National Park or of the water 30,000 feet deep in the Pacific Ocean. Microorganisms have been thriving in both of those locations.

Stanley Miller wrote in 1974, "We are sufficiently confident of our ideas about the origin of life that in 1976 a spacecraft will be sent to Mars to land on the surface with the primary purpose of the experiments being a search for living organisms."[15]

The Viking missions to Mars, two unmanned 7,700 pound spaceships mounted on Titan III E rockets, were launched from the Kennedy Space Center on August 20 and September 9 of 1975. Both of the Viking units contained a Mars-orbiting satellite and a lander vehicle. The orbiting portion was equipped with two-way communication equipment, computers, solar-energy panels, jet-propulsion engines and reservoirs of propellant fuel. The lander was a hexagonal-shaped three-legged aluminum structure which housed computers, power units, cameras and scientific instruments. Cruising through space at approximately 30,000 miles per hour, the first spaceship reached Mars after approximately 300 days of travel.

The spaceship was placed in orbit around the planet and potential landing sites were photographed. It was then that space scientists realized that the initial landing site chosen was too hazardous for a soft landing. Four weeks of intensive photographic search followed before a suitable landing site was located on the Chryse Planitia basin. Then on July 20, 1976, about 4 p.m. local Mars time, the *Viking I* touched down successfully near the designated site and began transmitting data back to earth.

---

[15]S. L. Miller, The Heritage of Copernicus, ed. Jerzy Neyman (Cambridge, MA: MIT Press, 1974), p. 328.

Model of the Viking lander #1 and #2 vehicles. These devices, weighing about 200 lbs, were equipped with propulsion rockets, a radioactive thermoelectric generator, nickel-cadmium rechargeable batteries, a 20-watt S-band transmitter, a computer and scientific equipment to study biology, chemical composition of the soil, meteorology, seismology and high resolution 360 degree cylindrical scan cameras.

A month and a half later, *Viking II* landed on Mars in a region known as Utopia Planitia, some 4,600 miles from the location of the first spaceship. The lander vehicles were equipped with sophisticated instruments such as a combination of gas chromatograph and mass spectrometer which could determine the composition of gaseous substances.

A mechanical arm scooped up some Martian soil and introduced it into an oven which baked the sample to increasingly higher temperatures. The soil was first heated to 302 °F to drive off volatile substances and water vapors were detected. Next, the temperature was raised first to 662 °F then to 932 °F. At these temperatures, all carbon-containing molecules break down to gaseous fragments, suitable for analysis by the gas chromatograph-mass spectrometer. The results of these experiments on both Viking landers were identical. Within the sensitivity of the instruments, ten parts per billion, no carbon-containing substances were found (all living matter contains organic carbon). By comparison, surface samples from the biologically destitute Antarctica, when similarly treated, yielded some organic matter at several thousand parts per billion.

The Viking landers performed other experiments, but their results were inconsequential. The billion-dollar question (the cost of the Viking missions in 1976 dollars): was there life on Mars in the past? The answer was a resounding NO.[16]

Analyzing the disappointing result, NASA scientists blamed the ultraviolet radiation-activated iron minerals as the chief culprits in preventing life from starting on Mars. They reasoned that perhaps there were life forms deeper in the soil.

Amidst all the analyses of the results of the Viking missions, there was not a single reference to the utter failure of Stanley Miller's self-assured predictions. It did not occur to anyone that the negative results were the fruits of faulty initial assumptions regarding how life comes to a planet. It is clear that no one at NASA accepts the Genesis account of Creation as truth.

Thus, the search for life on Mars continues at taxpayer's expense. In the year 2020 a new mission to Mars is planned, called "Mars2020." A robotic rover will be placed in the Jezero Crater on Mars, where there may have been a lake in the distant past, searching for signs of microbial

---

[16] G. A. Soffen and C. W. Snyder, "First Viking Mission to Mars," Science, August 27, 1976, pp. 759–765.

Photograph of the dry and dusty surface of Mars, taken by the Viking probe. These are the actual colors; the iron-rich soil and the salmon-colored sky.

life. It is not difficult to predict the outcome of this future expedition: another resounding failure!

Here on earth, origin of life research continues unabated. In 2005, Harvard University decided to solve the problem of life's origin on earth once and for all.[17] Pouring millions of dollars into the "Origin of Life Initiative," they hired the most brilliant young minds to tackle this problem. One of these scientists was Dr. David R. Liu, a young organic chemist with outstanding credentials. At the time of his hiring he made the following statement: "My expectation is that we will be able to reduce this [the origin of life] to a very simple series of logical events that could have taken place with no divine intervention."[18] Fourteen years later, with 171 publications and sixty-six patents to his name, there is still no word from him on how life originated on earth.

\*\*\*

On the sixth day of Creation the newly made biosphere was ready to receive its CEO, Adam. The Bible narrates that the Creator first formed an inert, lifeless Adam, and then breathed into his nostrils the "breath of life" (Gen. 2:7). We can only speculate what it must have been like for Adam to open his eyes and see the smiling face of his Creator bending over him.

> *Adam's intellect was immediately put to use. The Lord brought him pairs of newly-formed creatures and asked Adam to provide names for them.*

Unlike newborn babies, Adam came into the world a grown man, a mature person. He had immediate command of a language, complete with understanding complex concepts. Thus, the Creator could bring him up to speed without any delay, as to who he was and who the Creator was. It would not surprise us to see Adam bowing down before his Creator and with tears in his eyes thanking Him for bringing him into existence.

Adam's intellect was immediately put to use. The Lord brought him pairs of newly-formed creatures and asked Adam to provide names for them. Thus, the first man was immediately drawn into the Creation of the

---

[17] Alvin Powell, "Origin of Life to theorize about universe," The Harvard Gazette, https://1ref.us/17w (accessed 5/5/2020).
[18] Gareth Cook, "Project on the origins of life launched Harvard joining debate on evolution," Globe Staff, August 14, 2005.

Creation of Adam. "The Lord formed the man from the dust of the ground. He breathed the breath of life into the man's nostrils and the man became a living person" Genesis 2:7, NLT) This writer envisions the Creator crafting not merely a statue of Adam, but a clay figure, anatomically accurate to the level of cells. The "breath of life" first transmuted the inorganic clay into organic biomolecules of proteins, lipids, nucleic acids and carbohydrates, then started the biochemical engines in every one of the estimated 30 trillion cells of Adam's body.

new world. In addition, by a most subtle and gentle way, the Lord awakened in Adam the desire for a companion.

When the Creator saw that the strategy worked and Adam realized he was the only creature without a companion, He performed a surprising maneuver which we now recognize as a cloning procedure, Adam was anaesthetized and one of his ribs was removed. Using Adam's rib, the Lord cloned a second human, Eve. She was not an exact replica of Adam since she received a second X chromosome in place of his Y chromosomes, but Eve was truly Adam's twin!

The Lord did not really need Adam's rib and its DNA to create Eve since Adam's genetic information (as all of ours) was already in God's memory. But the cloning cemented Adam's relationship with Eve as nothing else could.

When Adam awoke from his sleep and saw Eve he was delighted, exclaiming, "[She] *is* now bone of my bones and flesh of my flesh" (Gen. 2:23, NKJV). In modern terms, Adam would have said, "She is my clone!"

Adam and Eve did not wear clothes in Eden, but they were not naked. Instead, they were covered with a soft light, preserving their privacy. If this sounds outlandish or unbelievable, we should remember that even today all of us are covered with light of the infrared variety, also known as heat. Every cell in our body (except red blood cells) contains mitochondria, organelles which are micro–furnaces generating heat. Adam and Eve's mitochondria produced much more energy than ours, and so the first humans radiated both heat and visible light.

The home of the first human couple, the ancestors of all humanity, was the Garden of Delight (Eden). It was a special estate expressly prepared for the first pair by the Creator. This garden must have been delineated from its surroundings by some form of barrier and one or more entry gates. Its dimensions are not known, but since it was to be cared for by one family, its size could not have been enormous, perhaps in the order of 50 to 100 acres.

The garden was populated with magnificent fruit-bearing trees, noble vines that could be trained, colorful bushes and clearings covered with a tapestry of flowers. A gently flowing, sparklingly clean river passed through the garden, providing water for the first couple to drink and for their hygienic needs.

In the center of Eden was a very special tree, the "tree of life" (Gen. 3:22). Biblical information is clear; although mankind was to exist in perpetuity, they were not created immortal! In order to sustain their lives, all

This scene from the beautiful Keukenhof Gardens in Netherlands hints of the all-surpassing splendor of the Garden of Eden.

humans were to eat the fruit of the tree of life![19] Adam and Eve, in fact, did eat this fruit while living in Eden. This is why the first human pair and their immediate descendants reached (from our perspective) spectacularly long ages.

Of all beings in the universe, only the Godhead is immortal. All creatures derive not only their origins from the Creator, but also their continual existence. The fruit of the tree of life, representing God's sustaining power, contains a substance needed for perpetual existence. What could this substance be? Increased understanding of the workings of living cells has given us a clue.

The twenty-three chromosomes of human cells, which appear as little sticks of various lengths under the microscope at appropriate magnification, all have caps at their ends called telomers. These caps protect the chromosomal strands from unraveling. Dr. Leonard Hayflick, working at the Wistar Institute in Philadelphia, Pennsylvania, in 1961, discovered that human cells cultivated in tissue cultures divide only forty to sixty times before they stop growing.[20] (This many cell divisions translate to approximately 120 years of human life!) Until then, it was believed that human cells divided an indefinite number of times. The cause for the finite number of cell division was traced to the shortening of the telomeric regions of the chromosomes at every cell division. When the telomeric regions of the chromosomes are near their ends, cells stop dividing. This is now believed to be the chief reason for aging.

Interestingly, embryos have active telomerase enzymes, which restore their telomers after each cell division, but at birth they cease to work. The fruit of the tree of life may have stabilized the telomerase enzymes, allowing them continued activity, restoring chromosomes to their full lengths after each cell division.

\*\*\*

Eden was to be a model for future generations of humans. It was the Creator's intention that the earth be populated by gardens where humans lived in close proximity to nature.[21]

\*\*\*

---

[19] Ellen G. White, Patriarchs and Prophets (Mountain View, CA: Pacific Press, 1890), p. 60.
[20] L. Hayflick, "The limited *in vitro* lifetime of human diploid cell strains," Experimental Cell Research 37 (1965): pp. 614–636.
[21] Ellen G. White, Education (Mountain View, CA: Pacific Press, 1903), p. 22.

By the time our solar system was created, the universe was likely in existence for a considerable time. While we have no information about the history of the cosmos prior to mankind's appearance, the presence of untold billions of galaxies strongly suggests that we are latecomers to the scene. As such, Adam and Eve had a lot of information waiting for them. From the outset, they received the most efficient, most complete instructions from angels and from the Creator Himself, who visited them frequently in their garden home. They heard the story of their creation from the Lord Himself. Likely, they were introduced to the accumulated wisdom of the civilizations of the universe, their arts, sciences and technologies. The first pair was also tasked to keep their garden abode in order by training the growing vines, harvesting, organizing and storing the abundance of fruits and nuts available to them. They were encouraged to study their environment, observing the behavior of creatures around them, learning everything they could about their fascinating world. Their lives in Eden were full of pleasant activities.

But Adam and Eve also discovered that not all was rosy with their world. Though the great Creator brought a brand new kind of planet into existence, unique to all creation and poised to bring excitement to the universe, its long-term future depended on a crucial choice by the first human pair.

They learned that the universe was in turmoil because the chief of angels, the "Light-bearer" (Lucifer), became dissatisfied with his status and imagined that the Godhead kept him from advancing to a state equal to the Creator (Isa. 14:12–14). No amount of earnest reasoning could change his mind and Lucifer became Satan, the adversary. He seduced one-third of the host of angels to join in rebellion against God. Lucifer also canvassed every created world searching for additional allies to his cause. None of the other worlds joined him.

Adam and Eve were warned of the machinations of Satan and they were informed that they too would have to choose whether to follow the Creator or Satan. They were strongly advised to stay together at all times to protect each other from being deceived by the enemy.[22]

Moreover, access to Adam and Eve by Satan was restricted to a limited "testing area" in the garden. Here, the Lord placed a marvelous-looking tree called "the tree of the knowledge of good and evil" (Gen. 2:9). This tree was loaded with exotic-looking, obviously delicious fruit.

---
[22] Ellen G. White, Patriarchs and Prophets (Mountain View, CA: Pacific Press, 1890), p. 53.

The test of loyalty to God consisted of staying away from the tree and refraining from eating its fruit. The penalty of disobedience was death!

This testing tree was not going to be a permanent fixture of the garden. After a probationary period of suitable length, it was going to be removed from Eden and then humanity would be forever safe from Satan's wiles.

Our world was meant to be an integral part of the community of created beings of the universe. Humans, bearing the image of the Creator both in outward resemblance and in character, were well suited to become special ambassadors of God to other created beings, assisting the Lord to forge new links with His creatures. Humanity was created not only to be gardeners on earth, but also to bless the universe.

\*\*\*

It is significant that the Bible begins with the story of origins. Everything else that follows makes sense only in the light of the Creation story. The Lord memorialized Creation by setting aside every seventh day. Clearly, it was important for mankind to remember the Creation event every week, even in Eden. Among the Ten Commandments, the fourth forbids secular labor on the seventh day as a way to imitate what the great Creator did during Creation week.

> *It is significant that the Bible begins with the story of origins. Everything else that follows makes sense only in the light of the Creation story.*

In our day, we recognize the benefit of not working on the seventh day as unquestionably beneficial for our physical and mental health. On this day, we get permission from a higher Power to stop our pursuit of professional and personal interests and seek a closer communion with God. In the Garden of Eden, Adam and Eve communed with the Lord face to face often. It is unlikely that they were exhausted by whatever physical labor they were engaged in. Yet, in spite of that, they were enjoined to change their routine on the seventh day! Continual awareness of their creaturehood was of supreme importance and the institution of the Sabbath assisted them in this.

\*\*\*

Words cannot describe the wonderful totality of being alive! Existence in the best sense of the word has no comparison to anything else. In a conversation with the Creator, Lucifer correctly described man's general attitude toward being alive: "Satan replied. 'A man will give all he has for his own life'" (Job 2:4, NIV). Being fully aware of the tremendous blessing of being alive, we would do well to extend our joy of living to everything and everyone in the biosphere. Such an attitude moves us to cherish every human being. After all, they are our blood relatives, descendants of Adam and Eve. Beyond that, every animal is a creature of the Lord and as such they have the right to be treated with compassion.

*** 

How old is the earth? The Bible not only informs us that earth, moon, sun and planets are all created entities, but also discloses their approximate age. In the absence of this information, we would likely join non-believers who declare the age of earth to be in the billions of years (See Appendix 1 for more details).

The key biblical text, which assists us in calculating the age of the earth, is 1 Kings 6:1, NKJV: "And it came to pass in the four hundred and eightieth year after the children of Israel had come out of the land of Egypt, in the fourth year of Solomon's reign over Israel … that he began to build the house of the Lord."

That year was 965 BC. Using this date and the biblical record, going backward all the way to Creation, we arrive at 3,896 BC as earth's birth date. This makes the earth 5,916 years old as of the year 2019. (See Appendix 2.)

Jewish people have observed Rosh Hashanah (the Jewish New Year) since biblical times. "Rosh Hashanah is also known as the Day of Remembrance, for on this day Jews commemorate the creation of the world, and the Jewish nation recalls its responsibilities as God's chosen people."[23] The year 2019, according to Jewish reckoning, is the year 5780, which is 136 years less than our biblical reckoning, a comparatively insignificant difference.

Supporting the biblical datum of origins is the significant fact that the oldest written historical records go back in time at the most 5,000–7,000 years![24] Naysayers counter with, "Homo sapiens have been around for more than two million years, but writing was invented only recently." How convenient an excuse!

The comparatively recent date for the earliest written material is matched by dates of the oldest civilizations in Mesopotamia, Egypt,

---

[23] The Editors of Encyclopaedia Britannica, "Rosh Hashana," Encyclopaedia Britannica, https://1ref.us/17x (accessed 5/5/2020).
[24] "History of Writing," Wikipedia, https://1ref.us/17y (accessed 5/5/2020).

Indus Valley, Shang (Yellow River Valley), Mesoamerica and Andean South America as well. They are all estimated to be less than 10,000 years old. Thus, historical records in general not only support the biblical presentation of human history, but they deny the plausibility of long evolutionary ages.

The Bible offers an important clue about our beginnings and this clue is all but ignored by those in the business of studying origins. It is clearly stated that the Creator called into existence a mature-looking biosphere. Adam and Eve were created as adults, the fruit trees of the Garden of Delight (Eden) were also mature and were loaded with fruits. The Lord presented to Adam fully developed male and female varieties of animals to be named. Everything on earth had an apparent age! What those ages were no one knows, but today's experts ignore the biblical record and start their calculations assuming a starting point of zero! Clearly, this is a mistake.

***

## The Fall of Mankind

At this time, earth and its immediate cosmic neighborhood is the slum of the universe. One could crisscross the vast expanse of the cosmos, traveling billions of light years without encountering another planetary system, where a star is orbited by eight planets; three of them rocky wastelands, four inert gas giants and a solitary blue globe covered with living organisms. Inhabitants in charge of this planet are ravaged by sickness, embroiled in violence and wars and their life spans are seldom more than 100 years. Ours is also the most primitive and technologically backward society in the universe. But superseding all these miseries is the overwhelming ignorance of the causes and remedies of these our conditions.

It is the Bible that explains the reasons for our sorry predicament.

***

We do not know how long Adam and Eve lived in the Garden of Eden. We can guess that it was fewer than nine months, the gestation time for a baby to be born. We learn from the Bible that the first child of Adam and Eve was born outside of the garden.

The turn of mankind's fortune for the worse happened within Eden. In plain language, Adam and Eve failed their test of loyalty to the Creator. It was not a spontaneous act, but the result of being victimized by the conniving enemy. Satan took control of the nervous system of a serpent resting on the branches of the testing tree. This organism became a medium of Satan, waiting to interact with Adam and Eve.

For reasons unknown, Eve wandered away from Adam's side in the garden. Of all the locations she could go, she found herself staring at the testing tree, loaded with beautiful-looking fruit. Was this just an unfortunate accidental event or was it the thought of tasting the forbidden fruit that intrigued Eve? If she was then expecting her first child, then Eve, as many expectant women, was craving exotic tastes.

As she was staring at the testing tree, Eve was startled to hear her thoughts articulated out loud by the serpent: ""Did God really say, 'You must not eat from any tree in the garden'?"" (Gen. 3:1, NIV). This seemingly silly question was a brilliant opening move in the ensuing match of wits. It put Eve at complete ease as the instructor of the foolish serpent. ""Of course we may eat fruit from the trees in the garden," the woman replied. "It's only the fruit from the tree in the middle of the garden that we are not allowed to eat. God said, 'You must not eat it or even touch it; if you do, you will die'"" (Gen. 3:2–3). Then the serpent took hold of the fruit from the tree and bit into it. (Side note: How could a snake "take a fruit" when snakes do not have arms and hands? Recently, a snake fossil was found with four limbs![25]) The serpent continued, "You see, nothing is happening to me. In fact, I can talk like you, because I ate this fruit. Don't worry, if you eat it, you will not die. The real reason God does not want you to eat this fruit is because if you taste this fruit, your eyes will be opened and you will become as wise as God Himself" (see Gen. 3:4–5).[26]

So, here at the very beginning of the Bible, we find an accurate articulation of the basis of Lucifer's rebellion. The great rebel accuses the Creator of keeping His creatures in ignorance of their true potential and preventing them from advancing to the same level as God. The underlying thesis is that every organism has the potential to move to a higher level of existence. The inventor of the theory of evolution was Lucifer!

The biblical record states that Eve believed the serpent and ate the forbidden fruit (Gen. 3:6). Feeling a strange exhilaration, she then found her husband and offered the fruit to him. Adam immediately realized what happened. Eve transgressed the expressed command of God and forfeited her right to life. Adam could not bear the thought of continuing

---

[25]D.M. Martill, H. Tischlinger and N.R. Longrich, "A four-legged snake from the Early Cretaceous of Gondwana," Science, July 24, 2015, pp. 416–419.
[26]Ellen G. White, Patriarchs and Prophets (Mountain View, CA: Pacific Press, 1890), pp. 54–56.

without his beloved Eve, the bone of his bone and flesh of his flesh. In a desperate act of self-sacrifice, he decided to end it all and die with Eve. He partook of the forbidden fruit.

What Adam did not grasp was that he held the fate of humanity in his hands. So long as he was faithful to the Creator, regardless of Eve's behavior, he and his future offspring were safe. But everything changed for the worse when he joined Eve in disobeying God.

The first human couple watched with dismay as the robe of light covering them slowly faded away. They felt the chill in the air and now they were naked. The forbidden fruit must have contained an inhibitory substance that degraded their mitochondrial energy output. Since we inherit mitochondria from our mothers, all future children were to live with weakened mitochondria.

Adam and Eve fabricated coverings for themselves from large leaves. It speaks well for their innate sense of ethics that they did not immediately kill animals for their skins. Adam and Eve were not going to afflict innocent, unsuspecting beings to benefit themselves.

When the first pair rebelled against their Creator, they incurred irreversible damage to the entire ecosystem. We now understand that the entire biosphere was created for the sake of mankind. With the fall of mankind into sin, the entire biosphere was victimized. On a larger scale, the current unfinished state of our solar system can also be understood to be the result of Adam and Eve's sin.[27]

It would have been easy for the Lord to stop Adam and Eve cold in their tracks before they foolishly ate the forbidden fruit. This action would have spared humanity 6,000 years of tragedy. But this was not an option. First, mankind's loyalty to the Creator had to be tested. Second, Adam and Eve were given absolute freedom to choose between God and Satan and to this day this choice is still ours to make.

*\*\**

After the initial excitement of eating the forbidden fruit wore off, Adam and Eve sensed that they were in big trouble. Deep in their souls they hoped that since this was their very first misdeed, maybe the Lord would cut them some slack.

Soon the Creator appeared in the Garden, and the pair hid from their best Friend. When the Lord called out to them, they replied with the

---

[27] G.T. Javor, "A Creationists View of the Solar System," Dialogue 27 (2005): pp. 13–15.

feeble excuse that they were embarrassed and afraid because they were naked—this, in spite of wearing coverings!

In time, they confessed to eating of the forbidden fruit. Adam, who a short time prior was willing to die rather than lose Eve, now explained, "The woman you put here with me—she gave me some fruit from the tree, and I ate it" (Gen. 3:12, NIV). That is, "I was minding my own business, when this creature whom You made (and thus, as her Manufacturer are partially liable for her behavior) essentially made me eat the forbidden fruit." Here we witness Adam articulating his innocence in this whole affair. How do we understand the less-than-stellar behavior of Adam, created perfect and sinless? Did eating the forbidden fruit cause a permanent change in Adam's character?

The Creator has endowed every organism, from bacterium to human, with a powerful survival mechanism. This capacity is dormant until a sense of danger activates it. Adam and Eve suddenly faced extinction and their excuses were clear manifestations that they did not want to die.

We are often told that we have a sinful, fallen nature inherited from Adam and Eve. If this were the case, sinful behavior would be genetic and there could be nothing done about it since we cannot alter our genes. Fortunately, this is incorrect.[28]

The universality of human sinfulness is caused by our tendency to be selfish. All sin can be traced to selfishness.[29] But what is selfishness? It is an exaggerated manifestation of self-preservation derived from the Creator's gift of survival mechanism. Our selfishness leads us to seek "survival" (i.e. get an advantage in whatever situation) at everyone else's expense. (The new "golden rule" is: "Do unto others before they do unto you!") But although our genes push us to take care of ourselves first, it is well in our power to be altruistic. Significantly, regardless of one's philosophical bent, self-denying behavior is a universally admired quality.

* * *

The Lord listened patiently to Adam and Eve's pathetic excuses and then pronounced His judgment. They were to leave the friendly confines of Eden and be denied any further access to the tree of life. Instead of dying immediately, they and all their descendants would live out their life spans in a far less friendly environment than Eden. Adam would have to wrestle

---

[28]G.T. Javor, "Does a Sin Gene Exist?" Ministry 82 ( January 2010): pp. 14, 15.
[29]Ellen G. White, Testimonies for the Church, vol. 4 (Mountain View, CA: Pacific Press, 1881), p. 384.

Adam and Eve were evicted from the Garden of Eden, so that they could no longer eat the fruit from the Tree of Life. The entrance to the Garden, guarded by an angel, became a place of worship for many antediluvians.

with the ground to grow crops and Eve would suffer pain when giving birth (Gen. 3:16–19).

But what was the point of allowing humanity to continue if the end for all was certain demise?

\*\*\*

At first blush, it seems strange and almost incomprehensible that a seemingly inconsequential act, such as eating a certain fruit in the Garden of Eden would precipitate these all-encompassing and tragic developments. How is it that a single event could sentence humanity and all other creatures in the biosphere to death? Could there not be a simple do-over? Could the Lord not tell Adam and Eve that their disobedience was unacceptable behavior and that one more such incident would be fatal to them?

We know that the laws of nature do not work this way. Touching live wires results in a shock every time, whether it was an accident or deliberate. Jumping off a high place will activate gravity every time. It is clear from the biblical account of our origins that this is how the universe operates. The consequences of our first parents' misbehavior simply could not be reversed without altering the order of the entire universe.

The first three chapters of Genesis describe the Creation of the world and mankind's fall from grace. The main theme of the rest of the Bible is a narrative of heaven's effort to reverse this disastrous beginning of humanity.

This is also where we discover the best news possible!—heaven's rescue plan for all humanity, the road to eternal, happy existence.

## The Redemption of Mankind

Apparently, humanity is redeemable. If it were not so, the Lord would have blotted out not only the earth and its inhabitants, but possibly the entire solar system.

To restore humanity into the community of sinless created beings, three problems had to be solved. First, the original sin of Adam and Eve had to be dealt with. Second, any further sin by individuals after Adam and Eve had to be made right. Third, humans needed to change from permanent sinners to permanent non-sinners. How is all that possible?

This is a puzzle with no obvious solution. How do we bypass the two moral laws of the universe? 1: Loving God with all our heart, mind and being. 2: Loving our fellow creatures as we love ourselves.

The shocking solution is so completely beyond human imagination and utterly mind-boggling that it will take eternity for us to process. In short, the mighty Creator of the universe becomes a human being, lives on earth a sinless life and accepts the punishment of death for the sins of Adam and Eve and for the entire human race. Our path to eternal life is soaked with the blood of Jesus!

The next chapter "A Recurring Nightmare," expands on this topic and points the way to eternal life.

## Chapter 3

# A Recurring Nightmare

For many years I had variations of the following dream: I would be standing by a bulletin board, looking at the schedules of final examinations posted under my name. Among the classes listed, invariably there would be one I did not remember registering for at the beginning of the semester. I therefore never attended a single lecture and now I was expected to take the final exam! I would wake up with deep anguish and a sense of helplessness at the prospect of being unprepared to answer questions and the certainty of flunking.

The Bible says: "For we must all appear before the judgment seat of Christ, that each one may receive the things *done* in the body, according to what he has done, whether good or bad" (2 Cor. 5:10, NKJV). It is a scary experience standing before a judge, even if we are innocent.

Something like this actually happened to me while in graduate school. I was growing cultures of the bacterium *Escherichia coli* in the Biochemistry Department of Columbia University at the Presbyterian Medical Center. I was getting ready to perform an experiment when I received a phone call. It was from the downtown New York City courthouse. "There is an outstanding jaywalking ticket here, made out to you and you have to come right away to take care of it. If you don't come within the hour, we will send a police officer to arrest you." So, even though it took days to prepare for

The judge's gavel is the emphatic period at the end of his sentence.

my experiment, I had to stop everything and take the subway to the courthouse. There I sat in a room with the judge, high on a platform, wearing a black robe dealing with one case after another. I was wracking my brain, vainly trying to remember getting a jaywalking ticket. Finally, I was called before the judge. A police officer testified that he issued a ticket years ago when there was a campaign in New York City to cut down on the number of people crossing streets in the middle of city blocks. He, of course, could not remember the face of the person. I asked to see the actual ticket and there I saw that the ticket was issued to someone who had my last name alright, but a different first name. When I pointed this out to the judge, he said that there would have to be a formal hearing where I would have to bring proper documents to prove who I was. He set the date for a few weeks hence.

At the appointed time, I stood before the judge with my citizenship paper, showing that I was not the person accused of jaywalking. The judge dismissed the charge against me and then said in parting, "… and don't jaywalk again!"

*\*\**

The prospect of standing before God to give account of everything that we have ever done or said should send shivers through our spines, but the Bible assures us that we need not be afraid of this event. In fact, this is the core of the best news possible! The Lord devised a fantastic plan to save humanity and at the same time, satisfy the immutable law of the universe. At the end, every sin must be accounted for and made right.

Shortly after being ushered out of Eden, the first pair was instructed to build an altar of stone and burn on it the carcass of an innocent lamb as an offering for their sins. Faithful followers of the Lord continued this practice of making sin offerings for thousands of years. We find the formal instructions regarding the details of sin offerings at the beginning chapters of the third book of the Bible, Leviticus: "If the animal you present as a burnt offering is from the herd, it must be a male with no defects. Bring it to the entrance of the Tabernacle so you may be accepted by the LORD. Lay your hand on the animal's head, and the LORD will accept its death in your place to purify you, making you right with him" (Lev. 1:3–4). Our sins separate us from the Lord. In order for God to accept us, an innocent Being has to die in our stead.

In ancient Israel, this process transferred the sins of everyone to the tabernacle. Then, once a year, on the Day of Atonement, the high priest entered the Most Holy Place of the tabernacle, carrying the blood of a kid goat. This compartment was a small, completely enclosed room containing the ark of the covenant, a cedar box holding the two stone tablets on which God Himself wrote the words of the Ten Commandments. Above the ark was the mercy seat, a golden slab (3.75' × 2.25') the same dimensions as the tablets of stone inside the ark, with two golden statues of cherubim at the two ends facing each other. The outstretched wings of the cherubim over the mercy seat touched one another. A continuous light shone between the angels, signifying God's presence. (There was no obvious source of the light, and this was thousands of years before the invention of electricity.) The high priest sprinkled the goat's blood onto the mercy seat, cleansing the sanctuary from a year's worth of Israel's sins. Finally, when the high priest emerged from the Most Holy Place, he confessed the sins of Israel onto the head of a second kid goat and this animal was sent away into the wilderness. While all of this was happening on the Day of Atonement, all activities stopped and everyone in Israel solemnly asked for the Lord's forgiveness.

Here we see the seriousness of sin and the length to which Israel of old was asked to go to gain forgiveness. But clearly, this could not be a permanent solution! After all, how could the death of innocent animals cancel human sins?

From our current perspective, we undertand that the practice of the sacrificial system for thousands of years was a forerunner of the actual, one-time sacrifice for all human sins, past and present. The millions of innocent animals killed to obtain divine forgiveness represented the Savior of the world. At one point in history, approximately 2,000 years ago, the Creator Himself appeared on earth as a human baby, lived a sinless life and died on a Roman cross on behalf of all humanity.

Prophets of old forecasted the coming of the Messiah, and for centuries the Hebrew people were anxiously awaiting His appearing. The expected Messiah was supposed to be a conqueror who would vanquish the oppressors of Israel and usher in a golden age, rivaling the days of great Solomon. Nothing of the sort happened. The Messiah turned out to be an itinerant Rabbi from Nazareth who spent His first thirty years in the carpenter shop of His earthly father, and then began His teaching and healing ministry. The identity of this Man is beyond fantastic, pushing human belief to almost beyond its limits! The biblical story declares this Person to be none other than the incarnate Creator of the universe (John 1:1, 3)! For what purpose did God become a human? To accept the penalty of Adam and Eve's sin and die in their stead (Isa. 53:5)!

At one point Jesus made reference to a curious incident of ancient Israel during their sojourn through the desert. This is the story as recorded in the book of Numbers:

> And the LORD sent fiery serpents among the people, and they bit the people; and much people of Israel died. Therefore the people came to Moses, and said, We have sinned, for we have spoken against the LORD, and against thee; pray unto the LORD, that he take away the serpents from us. And Moses prayed for the people. And the LORD said unto Moses, Make thee a fiery serpent, and set it upon a pole: and it shall come to pass, that every one that is bitten, when he looketh upon it, shall live. And Moses made a serpent of brass, and put it upon a pole, and it came to pass, that if a serpent had bitten any man, when he beheld the serpent of brass, he lived. (Num. 21:6–9, KJV)

This narrative holds the secret of the best news possible, the means by which mankind may live throughout eternity. The sinless, itinerant Rabbi, Joshua Ben Joseph (Jesus of Nazareth), who was lifted up on a Roman cross, is the focal point of our salvation. The apostle John puts it this way: "And as Moses lifted up the serpent in the wilderness, even so must the Son of Man be lifted up, that whoever believes in Him should not perish but have eternal life" (John 3:14–15, NKJV).

If by faith we accept the sacrifice of Jesus for our sins, the Bible assures us that we shall be saved! Believing that our sins are forgiven is a deeply personal act and no one can do it for us. As in the days of ancient Israel during the Day of Atonement, we are asked to examine our lives, confess our sins to the Lord in personal prayer, ask forgiveness in the name of the Messiah and sincerely believe that we are cleansed.

> *As in the days of ancient Israel during the Day of Atonement, we are asked to examine our lives, confess our sins to the Lord in personal prayer, ask forgiveness in the name of the Messiah and sincerely believe that we are cleansed.*

How many chances are we given to do this? There are no limits to the mercy of God. As long as there is life, there is hope. This is what the apostle John writes: "My little children, these things write I unto

Israelites bitten by fiery snakes, were instructed to look at the bronze serpent and be healed.

you, that ye sin not. And if any man sin, we have an advocate with the Father, Jesus Christ the righteous: And he is the propitiation for our sins: and not for ours only, but also for the sins of the whole world" (1 John 2:1–2, KJV).

In the course of our lives, we make a few "master decisions." We don't make them lightly because the consequences of these decisions are profound and largely determine how we are going to live. Examples of such decisions are: "Where am I going to live? How will I prepare for my life's work? Who will I marry?" Once we make a master decision, we don't revisit it every morning before rolling out of bed asking, for example, "Shall I go to work today, or not?" Each of us has a choice for one more master decision—to live or not to live forever in the kingdom of God! No one can stop us from looking to the uplifted Savior of the world for the forgiveness of our sins!

\*\*\*

That Jesus of Nazareth lived a sinless life for thirty-three years requires further discussion. How was it possible for Jesus to live a sinless life when every other human, from Adam on, sinned? Some churches baptize infants a few days after their birth, believing that at the moment of their birth they are guilty of the original sin of Adam and Eve and without baptism their eternal welfare is in jeopardy. There is no biblical basis for such a conclusion. We do not inherit the sins of our parents or ancestors. All babies are born innocent, sinless! When they cry or fuss, even if they inconvenience their parents, they are not doing anything sinister. They are simply communicating by the only means they have.

Of all newborn creatures, the human baby is the most helpless. Baby Jesus was not any different. The Creator of the cosmos, the all-knowing, mightiest Being in the universe came to earth in such a state. Somehow, He set aside all His powers and was born, being entirely dependent on His parents for sustenance, clothing and shelter. At first, He could only communicate by crying. The young Jesus had to learn to speak and needed instruction, as all infants do, about all aspects of life. From His mother, He learned the history of Israel, including the very words He spoke to Moses during their long journey through the wilderness. Still a child, Jesus puzzled out His true status and His true identity. By the age of twelve, during a customary family pilgrimage, He was in the temple in Jerusalem discussing profound religious topics with the leading rabbis of the time. When His parents reproached Him for being temporarily separated from them, Jesus spoke to the astonished Joseph and Mary referring to God as His father (Luke 2:49).

To be the spotless Sacrifice for all human sin, Jesus was called to accomplish what no other person was able to do. A single sin would have disqualified Him from His mission. Living in a town proverbial for its wickedness, He was subjected to every possible temptation. A disqualifying sin did not have to be heinous. An impatient response to an annoying request or lustful daydreaming could have qualified.

A sin by the Son of God would have nullified the plan of salvation that was set in motion immediately after the sin of Adam and Eve. It would have meant the end of mankind. But such an act also would have resulted in a breach among the members of the Godhead. This, in turn, would have jeopardized the very stability of the universe!

Thankfully, none of this happened. The Godhead deserves our eternal, deepest gratitude for taking such an extreme risk for hapless humanity.

## Chapter 4

# The History of Tomorrow

"Isn't it a shame that future generations can't be here to see all the wonderful things we're doing with their money?"[30] —Earl Wilson.

"The trouble with our times is that the future is not what it used to be."[31] —Paul Valery

The famous American sage, Yogi Berra, and at least a dozen other wise men are credited with the following observation: "It's tough to make predictions, especially about the future."[32]

How can future events be predicted when they have not yet taken place? Is it possible to foretell the future? There are many examples of spectacularly wrong predictions by persons of considerable expertise. Here are a few:

"To place a man in a multi-stage rocket and project him into the controlling gravitational field of the moon where the passengers can make scientific observations, perhaps land alive, and then

---

[30] "Earl Wilson Quotes," Brainy Quote, https://1ref.us/17z (accessed 5/5/2020).
[31] "Paul Valery," goodreads, https://1ref.us/180 (accessed 5/5/2020).
[32] "Yogi Berra," goodreads, https://1ref.us/181 (accessed 5/5/2020).

return to earth—all that constitutes a wild dream worthy of Jules Verne. I am bold enough to say that such a man-made voyage will never occur regardless of all future advances."[33] —Lee DeForest, American radio pioneer and inventor of the vacuum tube in 1926.

"The horse is here to stay but the automobile is only a novelty—a fad."[34] —The president of the Michigan Savings Bank advising Henry Ford's lawyer, Horace Rackham, not to invest in the Ford Motor Co, 1903.

"The world's potential market for copying machines is 5000 at most."[35] —Executive at IBM, to the eventual founders of Xerox, saying the photocopier had no market large enough to justify production, 1959.

"Fooling around with alternating current is just a waste of time. Nobody will use it, ever."[36] —Thomas Edison, American inventor, 1889 (Edison often ridiculed the arguments of competitor George Westinghouse for AC power).

"The wireless music box has no imaginable commercial value. Who would pay for a message sent to no one in particular?"[37] —Associates of David Sarnoff, responding to the latter's call for investment in the radio in 1921.

If experts can make spectacularly wrong guesses, what about the rest of us ordinary mortals? Truthfully, it is good news that the future is hidden from us. Certain knowledge of what will happen in the near or distant future would be a heavy burden to bear. Jesus says it best in the sermon on the mount, "Therefore do not worry about tomorrow, for tomorrow will worry about itself. Each day has enough trouble of its own" (Matt. 6:34, NIV).

In spite of all this, the Lord actually knows the future. For instance, we have the writings of Ellen White from the early 1900s:

> On one occasion, when in New York City, I was in the night season called upon to behold buildings rising story after story toward

---

[33]"Lee De Forest Quotes," Brainy Quote, https://1ref.us/182 (accessed 5/5/2020).
[34]"Worst Predictions," Fandom, https://1ref.us/183 (accessed 5/5/2020).
[35]"25 Famous Predictions That Were Completely Wrong," Blaze Press, https://1ref.us/184 (accessed 5/5/2020).
[36]Jamie Frater, "Top 30 Failed Technology Predictions," ListVerse, https://1ref.us/185 (accessed 5/5/2020).
[37]Chris Higgins, "Bad Predictions," Mental Floss, https://1ref.us/186 (accessed 5/5/2020).

heaven. These buildings were warranted to be fireproof, and they were erected to glorify their owners and builders .... The scene that next passed before me was an alarm of fire. Men looked at the lofty and supposedly fire-proof buildings and said: "They are perfectly safe." But these buildings were consumed as if made of pitch. The fire engines could do nothing to stay the destruction.[38]

What Mrs. White saw in night vision was the destruction of the World Trade Center skyscrapers in New York City on September 11, 2001, nearly 100 years into the future.

\*\*\*

The prophecies of the Bible demonstrate most convincingly that the Lord knows the future. We do not understand how this is possible, especially since the future is undetermined.

Among numerous examples, there is the towering prophecy about the entire history of the world, going forward to the second coming of Jesus. The fascinating backstory and the prophecy itself is narrated in the second chapter of the book of Daniel.

In the sixth century BC, the Neo-Babylonian Empire dominated the then known world. Its territory stretched from the Mediterranean and Red Sea to the Persian Gulf. In 597 BC, the kingdom of Judea rebelled against the rule of Babylon. In a punitive action, the Babylonian army captured Jerusalem and thousands of Jewish citizens were taken to Babylon, many of them youth belonging to the royal family and nobility. Among the captives were young Daniel and his three friends Hananiah, Mishael and Azariah (Dan. 1:1–6).

After a strenuous journey of some 400 miles on foot, the captives arrived in Babylon, the largest and most beautiful city of the ancient world, covering more than three square miles. It had an excess of 200,000 inhabitants. The walls around the city were considered, at one time, one of the seven wonders of the ancient world. Although various estimates of the height of the walls exist, there is agreement that the road on top of these walls was wide enough that a four-horse chariot could turn around. Entry to the city was through one of the eight magnificent gates.

The main gate, called Ishtar on the north side of the city, was built from bright blue glazed bricks. (It is reproduced in the Pergamon museum

---

[38]Ellen G. White, *Testimonies for the Church*, vol. 9 (Mountain View, CA: Pacific Press, 1909), pp. 12–13.

The magnificent city of Babylon, the capital of the neo-Babylonian empire in the 6th century BC.

in Berlin, Germany.) West of the Ishtar Gate were two fortified palace complexes that covered about forty acres.

The River Euphrates bisected the city into two equal halves, but a stone bridge solved this problem. Rising high on the imperial grounds was the Etemenanki ziggurat, the "House of the frontier between heaven and earth." It was a series of six raised platforms in a pyramid style, and a temple built for Marduk, the resident god of the city.

The streets were laid out on a grid, with the main axis parallel to the river. From the Ishtar gate ran a prominent boulevard, the Processional Way, a stone and brick paved avenue more than half a mile in length, leading the way from the palaces to the temples. The walls along this road were decorated with enameled lions.

It would have been entirely understandable if Daniel and his three friends abandoned their faith in God. All appearances suggested that Marduk was mightier than Jehovah. Why not join the conquerors and take the path of least resistance in life? Go with the flow.

These four young Hebrews, however, took an opposite course. They determined to be faithful to God, regardless of their dire circumstances. Under strict supervision, the young men were enrolled in an intensive multi-year training program to join the Babylonian civil servant class. They learned the Akkadian and Aramaic languages, the very elaborate cuneiform wedge writing system, Babylonian civil codes, science, mathematics, astronomy and the interpretation of dreams.[39]

Their food came from the King's kitchen, the best in the land. Nevertheless, because it was unclean from the perspective of the Hebrew youth, they indicated to their supervisor that they would prefer simple vegetables as their fare. The supervisor was reluctant to go along with their wishes, fearing that the young people under his charge would become sick. So Daniel and his friends proposed a test: For ten days they would eat only vegetables and then the supervisor could judge for himself whether their diet was adequate. The result was that Daniel and his friends appeared healthier than the rest of the group who ate the King's food. Consequently, they were allowed to continue with their chosen diet (Dan. 1:8–15).

\*\*\*

King Nebuchanezzar, the ruler of Neo-Babylon, had a miserable night of sleep. He tossed and turned and at the break of dawn summoned his brain

---
[39] Stephen Langdon, "A BABYLONIAN DREAM TABLET ON THE INTERPRETATION OF DREAMS," Penn Museum, https://1ref.us/187 (accessed 5/5/2020).

trusts and advisors, the magicians, enchanters, sorcerers and astrologers. He said to them, ""I have had a dream that deeply troubles me, and I must know what it means""" (Dan. 2:3).

*So this is what this is all about? No problem whatsoever!* the wise men must have thought. Solving the riddle of dreams and interpreting them was in their wheelhouse. Interpreting dreams was taught in the civil service preparatory school. "Books" of cuneiform tablets existed with extensive instructions on this subject. It was generally understood that dreams frequently contained important messages from gods. The next statement of the King, however, caught them by surprise, "[T]ell me the dream, and I shall know that you can give me its interpretation" (Dan. 2:9, NKJV).

The wise men spoke again, more or less ignoring what the King had just said, "Tell your servants the dream, and we will give the interpretation" (Dan. 2:4, NKJV). Those who have analyzed this story agree that the King's request was not a trick question. The monarch genuinely could not recall the details of his dream, although he was impressed that it was ominous and deeply significant. It was commonly held that if a person could not remember his or her dream, it was because the gods were angry with the individual.

> *It is worthy of note that the wise men, even in such a dire emergency, did not consult their deities for help. They knew it would be futile. Yet, they were correct when they pointed to the supernatural as the only possible place where the answers to the King's dilemma could be found.*

Let us imagine how the King felt. He has this cadre of people serving him, claiming to have special insight, knowledge and connection with the gods. It is for these unique abilities that the King has them on his payroll. Now they are asked to earn their keep and tell the King what the gods are saying to him. Is this such an unreasonable request? Apparently so! After some back-and-forth with the King and being threatened with utter destruction by him, and making no progress, the wise men blurt out that what they are asked to do has never been requested of wise men anywhere. What the King is asking is impossible for men! Only gods know these things.

When the King heard this insolent reply, he decreed the sentence of death on all wise men in Babylon (Dan. 2:12). Regardless, whether the wise men were conspiring against him or were telling the truth about their impotence, they did not deserve to live.

It is worthy of note that the wise men, even in such a dire emergency, did not consult their deities for help. They knew it would be futile. Yet, they were correct when they pointed to the supernatural as the only possible place where the answers to the King's dilemma could be found.

\*\*\*

Daniel and his three friends, though now part of the circle of Babylonian wise men since they successfully completed their course of study, were absent from the early morning meeting with the King. One had to belong to the top echelon of advisors to be invited to the palace in an emergency such as this. Daniel and his friends were newbies among the wise men.

Nevertheless, the sentence of death applied to all Babylonian wise men. Soon the commander of the King's guard appeared, possibly with a contingent of soldiers, to carry out the King's order—to kill Daniel and his friends and all the wise men.

Daniel met his potential executioner with a very reasonable question, "'Why has the king issued such a harsh decree?'" (Dan. 2:15). Arioch, the commander, then related to Daniel the entirety of the dramatic event that led the King to order the annihilation of his wise men. It was evident that the commander of the King's guard did not have any animosity toward Daniel, but he had an order to expedite. Daniel explained to Arioch that it would be best to delay the killings so that he could get help from his God concerning the riddle of Nebuchadnezzar's dream. The commander allowed Daniel to secure an appointment with the King where he, Daniel, could tell the King his dream and its interpretation.

At this point, Daniel had no knowledge of the King's dream; however, since he was facing certain death, he had nothing to lose by stepping out in faith. That night, following an earnest session of prayer by the four young men, Daniel received the secret of Nebuchadnezzar's dream in a dream of his own. Awakening, he could not refrain from praising God for His wisdom and power (Dan. 2:19–23).

Daniel hastened to Arioch, the chief executioner, to stop him from killing any of the wise men. "Take me to the king, and I will tell him the meaning of his dream," (Dan. 2:24) said Daniel.

Arioch did not waste any time. Although one did not just barge in to see the King without following the proper protocol, this was a happy emergency! "'I have found one of the captives from Judah who will tell the king the meaning of his dream!'" (Dan. 2:25) Arioch blurted out to the King.

It had been several days since the disturbing dream and its unpleasant aftermath. It is not difficult to guess that since the dismissal of his wise men, the King spent every waking moment vainly trying to recall fragments of his dream. As the ruler of the then known world, commanding all possible means and power, he was completely unaccustomed to this foreboding sense of helplessness.

The King turned to Daniel, who accompanied Arioch and said, "'Is this true? Can you tell me what my dream was and what it means?'" (Dan. 2:26). Daniel replied,"There are no wise men, enchanters, magicians, or fortune-tellers who can reveal the king's secret. But there is a God in heaven who reveals secrets, and he has shown King Nebuchadnezzar what will happen in the future. Now I will tell you your dream and the visions you saw as you lay on your bed" (Dan 2:26–28). Wow! Daniel had the King's full and undivided attention.

Daniel began, "As you lay on your bed, O king, your thoughts turned to the future, and the Revealer of Mysteries made known to you what will happen" (Dan. 2:29, BSB).

\*\*\*

As this dramatic story is told, we usually pass quickly by the introduction to get to the main part where the future is described. We may miss the astounding implication of what Daniel just said. Here was the young captive from Judah who revealed what the King's thoughts were! How was this possible?

The clear implication is that the great God of heaven scans our brains and reads our thoughts, most likely constantly, and when appropriate, responds to or acts on them. There are more than 7 billion heads currently on earth that require such attention. Is this not too much for the Lord? Clearly not! God says to Jeremiah, "'Behold, I *am* the Lord, the God of all flesh. Is there anything too hard for Me?'" (Jer. 32:27, NKJV)

Scientists now have the ability to scan our brains, using formidable machines to do magnetic resonance imaging (MRI), computer tomography (CT) and positron emission tomography (PET).

The human brain is by far our most complex organ. It contains at least 100 billion cells (neurons). The connections between neurons are called synapses. Each brain cell has an average of 7,000 connections to other neurons. The brain of a three-year-old child has about 1,000 trillion connections. This number declines with age, stabilizing by adulthood. Estimates for an adult range from 100 to 500 trillion synapses. Every thought results in the activation of a series of neurons. Our thoughts, feelings and memories are somehow dependent on the networks of synapses formed in our brains. With the use of appropriate radioactive isotopes, PET scans can show areas of high metabolic activity in the brain. But this is the extent of it. Even our most sophisticated technologies are incapable of identifying a single thought!

Contrast all of this with what the Lord says about His ability to look at people's thoughts: "I, the LORD, search the heart, I test the mind, even to give every man according to his ways, according to the fruit of his doings" (Jer. 17:10, NKJV).

*\*\*\**

Daniel continued:

> In your vision, Your Majesty, you saw standing before you a huge, shining statue of a man. It was a frightening sight. The head of the statue was made of fine gold. Its chest and arms were silver, its belly and thighs were bronze. Its legs were iron, and its feet were a combination of iron and baked clay. As you watched, a rock was cut from a mountain, but not by human hands. It struck the feet of iron and clay, smashing them to bits. The whole statue was crushed into small pieces of iron, clay, bronze, silver and gold. Then the wind blew them away without a trace, like chaff on a threshing floor. But the rock that knocked the statue down became a great mountain that covered the whole earth.
>
> That was the dream. Now we will tell the king what it means. Your Majesty, you are the greatest of kings. The God of heaven has given you sovereignty, power, strength, and honor. He has made you the ruler over all the inhabited world and has put even the wild animals and birds under your control. You are the head of gold.
>
> But after your kingdom comes to an end, another kingdom, inferior to yours, will rise to take your place. After that kingdom has fallen, yet a third kingdom, represented by bronze, will rise to rule the world. Following that kingdom, there will be a fourth one, as strong as iron. That kingdom will smash and crush all previous

A representation of what the frightening image in Nebuchadnezzar's dream may have looked like. It's head was gold, its chest silver, its thighs bronze, its legs iron, and its feet a mixture of iron and clay.

empires, just as iron smashes and crushes everything it strikes. The feet and toes you saw were a combination of iron and baked clay, showing that this kingdom will be divided. Like iron mixed with clay, it will have some of the strength of iron. But while some parts of it will be as strong as iron, other parts will be as weak as clay. This mixture of iron and clay also shows that these kingdoms will try to strengthen themselves by forming alliances with each other through intermarriage. But they will not hold together, just as iron and clay do not mix.

During the reigns of those kings, the God of heaven will set up a kingdom that will never be destroyed or conquered. It will crush all these kingdoms into nothingness, and it will stand forever. That is the meaning of the rock cut from the mountain, though not by human hands, that crushed to pieces the statue of iron, bronze, clay, silver, and gold. The great God was showing the king what will happen in the future. The dream is true, and its meaning is certain. (Dan. 2:31–45)

The King listened to Daniel, spellbound. When the Hebrew youth finished speaking, the King rose from his throne and threw himself at the feet of Daniel in an act of worship (Dan 2:46). Nebuchadnezzar clearly understood that God Himself spoke to him through Daniel. The King was overwhelmed with gratitude.

\*\*\*

From history books we find that the Neo-Babylonian empire lasted from 605 BC until 539 BC. It was followed by the Medo-Persian empire from 539 BC until 331 BC. Next came the Greece-Macedonian empire from 331 BC until 146 BC. It was followed by the Roman empire from 146 BC until AD 476. There has not been a world empire since then and, according to Daniel's prophecy, there never will be one.

Since the fall of the Roman empire in AD 476, we have been living in the "toes" of the statue of King Nebuchadnezzar's dream where we have strong and weak countries interspersed around the world. The uncannily accurate description of future events, such as found in the story of Nebuchadnezzar's dream in Daniel chapter 2, has caused many detractors to claim that the book was written much later than the sixth century BC, possibly 400 years later. However, here are a few facts to strengthen the authenticity of the book of Daniel.

Daniel describes Nebuchadnezzar as the builder of Babylon. By 160 BC, this information was lost. Instead, Greek historians mistakenly claimed that Babylon was built by the legendary Assyrian queen, Semiramis.

When Daniel was old, an incident took place (described in Daniel chapter 5) where Daniel interpreted the writing on the wall by a mysterious hand during Belshazzar's last feast. As a reward, the King offered Daniel third place in his kingdom. We now know that he could give Daniel only the third place in the kingdom since Belshazzar was a co-regent with his father, Nabonidus. This information was also lost by 160 BC, but Daniel had the politics right.

The Book of Daniel was found among the Dead Sea Scrolls dating from about 125 BC. There are several fragments and they do not all agree. In other words, there were different "schools" of documents, one close to the Masoretic Text (a copy of the Hebrew Bible considered the authority because it is the source for most translations of the Old Testament), and one nearer the Septuagint (the Greek translation of the Old Testament). It is impossible for such "schools" of texts to have developed in only forty years or less. The book of Daniel, therefore, must be more ancient.

The prophecy in Daniel chapter 2 predicts history until the end of the world. Thus, it cannot be claimed that it is simply a faux-prophecy, written after the fact. This biblical information should shock our contemporary secular activists. Climate change and global warming will not make earth uninhabitable and are not factors in the closing of earth's history.

\*\*\*

Although the prophecy in the second chapter of Daniel covers history until the end of time, the details become fuzzy the farther away it moves from the sixth century BC. It provides hardly any insight about our time except an assurance that we are living in the last segment of human history. With regard to that, this is exactly what the apostle Paul believed almost 2,000 years ago.

To bring the twenty-first century into sharper focus, we need to return to the story of the Messiah's death on the Roman cross. The gospels describe the tragic events of Jesus' crucifixion and death on Passover Friday. The most detailed description is found in the gospel of John, chapter 19.

Joseph of Arimathea obtained permission to take the tortured body of Jesus off the cross and place it in his own tomb in a garden, near the site of the crucifixion. As it was close to sundown on Friday, Christ's body was

The empty tomb of Jesus.

hastily wrapped in long linen sheets, along with spices of myrrh and aloes (John 19:38–42).

Then followed the worst Sabbath of the disciples' lives, filled with dark foreboding, bitter disappointment and heart-wrenching sorrow. But at sunrise the next day, Sunday morning, when the female followers went to the tomb to complete Friday's hasty burial, they found the tomb empty. Inside lay the spice-bearing burial cloths neatly folded. Two young men dressed in dazzling white outfits appeared and informed them that Jesus had risen from the dead. The ladies promptly notified some of Jesus' disciples and they rushed to the tomb and confirmed the ladies' report (Luke 24:1–10; John 20:1–8).

> *During the next forty days, the resurrected Lord taught His disciples the meaning of His life and death. He commissioned His followers to teach everyone the best news possible: eternal life for all who accept the Lord's sacrifice for their sins.*

During the next forty days, the resurrected Lord taught His disciples the meaning of His life and death. He commissioned His followers to teach everyone the best news possible: eternal life for all who accept the Lord's sacrifice for their sins.

After forty days, Jesus left earth in a spectacular fashion, described in the book of Acts, chapter 1:

> After saying this, he was taken up into a cloud while they were watching, and they could no longer see him. As they strained to see him rising into heaven, two white-robed men suddenly stood among them. "Men of Galilee," they said, "why are you standing here staring into heaven? Jesus has been taken from you into heaven, but someday he will return from heaven in the same way you saw him go!'" (Acts 1:10–11)

Here we see the Bible holding a magnifying glass over the scene in Nebuchadnezzar's dream, where a stone cut from a mountain, not by a human hand, smashes up all of the kingdoms of earth. The stone flying at the statue is nothing less than the return of Jesus, His second coming! In the sixth century BC, such detail would have been thoroughly incomprehensible.

Before Jesus commenced His ministry, the Lord raised up a prophet of extraordinary capabilities, John the Baptist. He called everyone to repent of their sins and be baptized. He subsequently introduced Jesus as the "Lamb of God" (John 1:36). Thus, it seems reasonable that the Lord would raise up a movement also, to heighten awareness of the nearness of the second coming of Jesus.

Beginning in the 1820s, William Miller, a Baptist minister, became convinced that the second coming of Jesus was at hand. His studies of the prophecies in the book of Daniel placed the date of Jesus' coming at October 22, 1844. The news of this date spread like wildfire, not only in this country, but also in Europe. Growing up in communist Hungary in the 1950s, I remember reading a story in elementary school about strange Hungarians who, in the 1840s, abandoned their farms and crops, waiting for Jesus to come.

The Millerite movement in the USA had anywhere from 50,000 to 100,000 followers.[40] When Jesus did not return on October 22, 1844, the Millerite movement collapsed. Most people returned to their former churches, but small groups of believers decided to continue their Christian fellowship. The Seventh-day Adventist Church, officially founded in 1863, was one of these organizations. As of this writing, with a worldwide membership of approximately 20 million, they continue to work in their communities by emphasizing healthy living, the sacredness of all ten of God's commandments, the best news possible (traditionally known as the gospel) and the soon return of Jesus. As the twelfth largest religious body in the world, the Seventh-day Adventist Church is ethnically and culturally diverse and maintains a missionary presence in over 215 countries and territories. The church operates over 7,500 schools, including over 100 post-secondary institutions, numerous hospitals and publishing houses worldwide.[41]

The Seventh-day Adventist Church views its main task as alerting people to the nearness of the second coming of Jesus. While they do not set dates, they call attention to the prophecies of the Bible which point to our time as the time when Jesus will return.

---

[40]The Editors of Encyclopaedia Britannica, "William Miller," Encyclopaedia Britannica, https://1ref.us/17x (accessed 5/5/2020).
[41]"Seventh-day Adventist Church," Wikipedia, https://1ref.us/188 (accessed 5/5/2020).

The Second Coming of Jesus.

## Chapter 5

# Eternal Bliss

A story is told of a tourist who decided to visit as many churches as he could in all fifty states of the USA. Shortly after beginning his journey, he was surprised to find a pay phone in the lobby of every church. Under each phone was the sign "Direct Line to Heaven! $10,000 per minute." When the tourist arrived in Texas, the first church he found also had a pay phone in the lobby, but it had a different sign "Direct Line to Heaven! 25 cents/minute." The tourist went to see the pastor of the church and asked about the sign under the pay phone. The pastor explained the sign to the tourist, "You see, it is a local call!" (See also Appendix 3.)

\*\*\*\*

The following is the last paragraph of the monumental book, *The Great Controversy* by Ellen G. White:

> The great controversy [between Christ and Satan] is ended. Sin and sinners are no more. The entire universe is clean. One pulse of harmony and gladness beats through the vast creation. From Him who created all, flow life and light and gladness, throughout the realms

of illimitable space. From the minutest atom to the greatest world, all things, animate and inanimate, in their unshadowed beauty and perfect joy, declare that God is love."[42]

All of us are invited to be on the earth made new and by God's grace this can be a reality indeed! This is what *The Best News Possible* is all about!

Augustine of old wrote, "We were made for You, O Lord, and our heart is restless until it rests in you."[43] Currently our sins block us from experiencing the physical presence of the Lord. This will no longer be the case. Seeing Jesus face-to-face and hearing His gentle voice will surpass all wonder and joy!

> *Currently our sins block us from experiencing the physical presence of the Lord. This will no longer be the case. Seeing Jesus face-to-face and hearing His gentle voice will surpass all wonder and joy!*

We are encouraged here on earth to open our hearts and talk with the Lord as to a friend,[44] but on the new earth we will hear the Lord's immediate reply! When we express our joy at being in His presence, He will tell us of His pleasure in communing with us face-to-face. We will respond by assuring Him that He is everything to us and that we will love Him throughout eternity! The Lord will show us the great city He has prepared for us. Angels will take us to our personal quarters in the city. It is likely that those who suffered the most for their faith will live nearest to the throne of God, the source of constant light.

In the book of Revelation, we read, "To everyone who is victorious ... I will give to each one a white stone, and on the stone will be engraved a new name ..." (Rev. 2:17). It will be an everlasting, personal gift and our most precious possession. We will also receive a golden crown, inscribed with our new name and the phrase, "Holiness to the Lord."[45] "And now the prize awaits me—the crown of righteousness, which the Lord, the righteous Judge, will give me on the day of his return. And the prize is not just for me but for all who eagerly look forward to his appearing"

---

[42]Ellen G. White, The Great Controversy (Mountain View, CA: Pacific Press, 1911), p. 678.
[43]St. Augustine of Hyppo: Confessions. Lib 1, 1–2, 2.5, 5: CSEL 33, 1–5.
[44]Ellen G. White, Steps to Christ (Mountain View, CA: Pacific Press, 1892), p. 93.
[45]Ellen G. White, The Great Controversy (Mountain View, CA: Pacific Press, 1911), p. 645.

(2 Tim. 4:8). Portable harps will be waiting for us, and we will all become harpists of sorts.[46]

\*\*\*

What will be the language of the new earth? Will it be the same as spoken at the beginning of earth's history? It would stand to reason that it would be the tongue spoken throughout the vast universe. Undoubtedly, the redeemed will speak and understand this language. It is unlikely that it is one of the hundreds of tongues now spoken on earth.

\*\*\*

As we go through life, we change a little every day. This is because our brain records the day's events, conversations and thoughts, and then adds them to our memory bank. Augmentation of our memory bank, in turn, changes us. The question is: if we are fortunate enough to be admitted to the new earth, which version of ourselves will be there? Or will we appear as new, sanitized versions of our old selves masquerading as us?

None of us can do any better than that rich, cranky old man in the beginning story of this book who could not take his money with him to the grave and beyond. Surprisingly, however, we all will take our most precious possessions with us to the new earth—our memories, thoughts, opinions and personalities. Our character!

> *Our testimonies about our life histories and our spiritual journeys will be of great interest to the residents of the universe. They also will testify to the efficacy of the unfailing love of our Redeemer.*

The plan of salvation works only if it is the actual, former sinner who appears on the new earth. Our testimonies about our life histories and our spiritual journeys will be of great interest to the residents of the universe. They also will testify to the efficacy of the unfailing love of our Redeemer. After all, we have been rescued from eternal destruction by the blood of God's Lamb and we will have as many different personal testimonies to share as there are saved humans.

\*\*\*

---

[46]Ibid.

Early in the Bible we are introduced to the "for the sake of…" principle. In a touching episode, described in chapter 18 of the book of Genesis, we find Abraham bargaining with the Lord for the lives of Sodom's residents. This city was legendary for its wickedness and the Lord Himself came to visit it.

On the way to Sodom, the Lord stopped by Abraham's home and revealed to him the upcoming doom of Sodom. Abraham asked the Lord, ""Suppose you find fifty righteous people living there in the city—will you still sweep it away and not spare it for their sakes?"" (Gen. 18:24) The Lord answered, ""If I find fifty righteous people in Sodom, I will spare the entire city for their sake"" (Gen. 18:26). Abraham then asked if there would be only forty, then thirty, then twenty and finally ten righteous people in the city, would the Lord still spare them? (Gen. 18:29–32)

The Lord answered in the affirmative every time. Abraham was finally satisfied. His nephew, Lot, and his family lived in Sodom and surely there would be ten righteous men and women among them! Unfortunately, Abraham was too optimistic. Sodom, in fact, went up in smoke, but not before Lot and his two daughters were rescued.

Elsewhere in the Bible, we find Laban, Jacob's father-in-law, telling Jacob: "The LORD has blessed me for your sake" (Gen. 30:27, NKJV). In Genesis 39:5, NKJV, we read, "[T]he Lord blessed the Egyptian's [Potiphar, the captain of the guards] house for Joseph's sake …"

Based on these and other examples in the Bible, I believe that the Lord will bring people into the new earth for the sake of some of His beloved children. Who would not like to experience the warmth of human love among family and friends throughout eternity? And could we experience joy, spending eternity without our parents, siblings, spouses and children? Would we not mourn their absence forever? Anticipating the bliss of eternal life, we would do well to assume that we will be surrounded by our loved ones through eternity! Would not the Lord do this for our sake?

\*\*\*

There will be many people on the new earth who, at first, have no idea where they are and how they got there. Among them will be the victims of the Holocaust, 6 million Jews murdered for their "crime" of being the descendants of Abraham, Isaac and Jacob. This horrendous calamity led many conscientious Jews to abandon their faith in God, and still others to

A portion of a Holocaust Monument by the Danube river in Budapest, Hungary. It displays shoes of innocent Jewish victims, shot into the river by thugs of the infamous "Arrow Cross" party in the winter of 1944.

turn from observant Jews to agnostics. What can be done to make right these unspeakable atrocities? Justice demands punishment of the perpetrators, but even that does not help the victims.

After World War II the newly formed government of Germany assumed responsibility for the Holocaust, and began payments to the families of the deceased. Humanly speaking, nothing more could be done! But there is a God in heaven who is able to do much more to make everything right!

I believe that every Jew who perished during the Holocaust was a martyr. The new world, characterized by the apostle Peter as a place where God's righteousness reigns (2 Peter 3:13), would not be complete without all the resurrected martyrs of the Holocaust.

\*\*\*

In the final analysis, it is the all-wise and all-knowing Creator who determines who will live on the new earth. The Bible assures us that every one of us is eligible, and the best news possible is that we do not have to do anything heroic, only look to the Savior uplifted on the cross and ask for the forgiveness of our sins!

\*\*\*

None of us will gain admittance to the new earth because of our own merits. As far as our characters are concerned, the prophet Jeremiah's characterization applies: "Can an Ethiopian change the color of his skin? Can a leopard take away its spots? Neither can you start doing good, for you have always done evil" (Jer. 13:23).

It will be of great help on the new earth that there will be no threat of calamity, material loss, illness or death. We will be in the ultimate safe environment. Moreover, we will benefit from the presence of helpful, selfless angels and beings from elsewhere in the cosmos.

Yet, a lifetime of looking out for number one does not go away easily! We will have our work cut out to become more like our Savior! It would not be a surprise to learn that programs have been created, tailored to our individual personalities, temperaments, and histories. These combine theoretical and hands-on learning, designed to facilitate our becoming more unselfish and more loving members of the new world order.

\*\*\*

Among the resurrected will be Adam, the progenitor of all humanity. Jesus will take him to a very special place on the new earth, the same garden where Adam lived before sin. There, Adam will recognize the very vines he trained and the trees whose fruits he gathered. Jesus will take him to the tree of life, pluck a fruit from it and give it to Adam to eat. Adam, in turn, will eat of the fruit and embrace Jesus in heartfelt gratitude for all of God's goodness to him and all of Adam's offspring.[47]

We know of a few other outstanding humans who will be on the new earth. Enoch of old, who walked with God, the great Moses and the prophet Elijah who was whisked to heaven in a fiery chariot. In a vision, Ellen White saw Abraham, Isaac, Jacob, Noah and Daniel in heaven.[48] Also there will be the twelve apostles, as the twelve foundation stones of the walls of the New Jerusalem will bear their names (Rev. 21:14). New Jerusalem, the capital of the new earth and the new center of the universe, will be a Jewish city, as its twelve gates will be named after the twelve tribes of Israel (Rev. 21:12).

The city itself will have many streets, parks, squares, lakes and other places of interest. The crystal clear water of the river of life will flow in the middle of the main street (Rev. 22:1–2). Undoubtedly, every facet of the city will have a unique name, perhaps honoring worthies.

*\*\*\**

What is referred to by the prophets as gold—the streets of the New Jerusalem, the crowns of the redeemed, etc.—will be most likely some alloy of gold and other metals. Pure gold is soft, heavy as lead and wears away in a short time. Neither is gold transparent. Crowns made from pure gold could not be kept on one's head comfortably for any length of time.

*\*\*\**

"And he said to me, These are they which came out of great tribulation, and have washed their robes, and made them white in the blood of the Lamb" (Rev. 7:14, KJV).

Whereas Adam and Eve were covered with robes of light in the original Garden of Eden, the Bible places the redeemed in white robes. While in biblical times robes were stylish and elegant garments, in our times they are less so. Projecting forward to the new earth, we should keep an open

---
[47] Ellen G. White, The Great Controversy (Mountain View, CA: Pacific Press, 1911), p. 648.
[48] Ellen G. White, Selected Messages, vol. 1 (Washington, DC: Review and Herald, 1958), p. 64.

Resurrected children will grow up on the New Earth in the company of angels and the Creator Himself.

mind as to the styles of apparel worn there. We may be certain, though, that our clothing will enhance our appearance without gaudiness. Males and females will likely have differing styles and colors.

When contemplating what life will be like on the new earth, an important question is the relationship between males and females. Since our gender is built into our fabric, if we lost it upon resurrection we would not be our authentic selves!

One of the so-called "hard sayings" of Jesus on this topic is recorded in the gospel of Luke: "Jesus answered and said to them, "The sons of this age marry and are given in marriage. But those who are counted worthy to attain that age, and the resurrection from the dead, neither marry nor are given in marriage; nor can they die anymore, for they are equal to the angels and are sons of God, being sons of the resurrection" (Luke 20:34–36, NKJV).

Jesus is cautioning us not to expect to find romance and marriage on the earth made new. However, there does not seem to be any reason why resurrected, happily married (on earth) couples could not continue their close friendships throughout eternity.

\*\*\*

There is no information anywhere about the nitty-gritty of everyday life on the earth made new. This is both good and bad.

The good: From the perspective of the inquiring mind, it is irresistible to imagine and innovate on paper.
The bad: Chances are that we are wrong!

The apostle Paul put a damper on any conjecture regarding this topic: "But as it is written, Eye hath not seen, nor ear heard, neither have entered into the heart of man, the things which God hath prepared for them that love him" (1 Cor. 2:9, KJV).

When we read that the inhabitants of the new world will be wearing robes, we immediately wonder, where did these robes come from? Who designed them and who manufactured them? Since we are talking about eternity, it would stand to reason that individuals will need more than one robe. What about appropriate apparel for various occasions, attending worship services, attending solemn assemblies, working in the field or traveling? Undoubtedly, the new earth will be far cleaner than our present environment, but our clothes will soil sooner or later. What will heaven's solution be to keep our clothes clean? A more basic question is, Will there be factories which manufacture apparel? And ... who will work there? These questions are merely the tip of the iceberg. For everyday existence we now need hundreds of essential items. Which ones of these will we need on the new earth? Fortunately, we do not have to stay awake at night worrying about minutia like these. We have Jesus' words on this topic: ""So don't worry about these things, saying, 'What will we eat? What will we drink? What will we wear?' These things dominate the thoughts of unbelievers, but your heavenly Father already knows all your needs"" (Matt. 6:31–32).

*\*\**

We may assume that our metabolism will be similar to what we have now, except perhaps more efficient. With the help of fully functioning telomerase enzymes (having eaten the fruit from the tree of life), we will not experience any aging. We will require food and water and, naturally, there will have to be sanitary solutions to our bodily waste.

Interestingly, none of the visions of the new earth contain any reference to transportation. One reason for this may be that transportation technologies will be so different from what we now have that it would needlessly confuse and frighten the recipient of the revelation. Still, we may be certain that whatever the means of getting around on the new earth, it will not be airplanes, trains or automobiles!

*\*\**

Our solar system is 3.5 light years (25.8 trillion miles) from the Alpha Centauri star system, our nearest neighbor in the Milky Way Galaxy. Traveling at 50,000 miles per hour, the speed of our fastest space probe, a one-way journey there would take 58,900 years.

Angels are not bound by cumbersome travel as we are. Consider the following from the book of Daniel: "As I was praying, Gabriel, whom I had seen in the earlier vision, came swiftly to me at the time of the evening sacrifice. He explained to me, "Daniel, I have come here to give you insight and understanding. The moment you began praying, a command was given. And now I am here to tell you what it was, for you are very precious to God" (Dan. 9:21–23). We do not know where the angel Gabriel was when he received word from the Lord to come to earth and visit the prophet Daniel.

Daniel's prayer could not have lasted more than fifteen minutes. We do not have any concept that could explain Gabriel's instantaneous notification of Daniel's need and the angel's ability to appear at Daniel's side within minutes. But here we get a glimpse of the magnificence of heaven's technology. Thus, we can be confident that there will be no transportation problems whatsoever on the new earth.

\*\*\*

We are so used to living in a stressful environment that we would be completely disoriented if all our stresses suddenly went away. Stress is like gravity—it keeps us firmly centered on our limitations and problems. We all deal with frustrations of not having enough strength, resolve, skills or money to accomplish our goals while coexisting with others who do not always treat us as we would like to be treated. We deal with dwindling years, failing health and diminished resources. Thus, it is almost impossible to project ourselves, in thought, into a completely stress-free world where we will be free of the limitations frustrating us now.

I can think of only one thing that could cast a shadow over the joy of being on the new earth. It is the possibility that one or more of our loved ones here on earth will not be with us on the earth made new. The reality is that we do not have the power to force others, even loved ones, to believe and act as we do. However blissful and happy we may think life on the new earth may be, it is also possible that some people would be uncomfortable, if not miserable, in such an environment. Would we wish that these loved ones be sentenced to discomfort for eternity? Some on the new earth will have to come to terms with such circumstances.

\*\*\*

We are so constituted that we are not able to sustain emotional highs or lows for extended periods. But even as we project ourselves into the fairytale-like new earth where everything is perfect, knowing our own emotional makeup, we have to be prepared for some emotional down time. Yet, we will always be perfectly happy and content. We are assured that there will be no pain on the new earth. The Bible says in the book of Revelation, "And God shall wipe away all tears from their eyes; and there shall be no more death, neither sorrow, nor crying, neither shall there be any more pain: for the former things are passed away" (Rev. 21:4, KJV). Yet, we would expect pain on the new earth if we stubbed our toes. Without the sensation of pain we would be like the lepers.

\*\*\*

Surpassing the peace and joy of experiencing the new earth will be worshipping our dear Lord face to face. We will be standing on a glass-like shiny surface before the throne of God (Rev. 4:6), singing, playing our harps and expressing our heartfelt love toward our Creator and Redeemer. Worship time will be filled with joyous celebration and praise. He will hear our individual words and will respond to every one of us, assuring us that He heard our thanks and praises. Even though we will be part of a great throng, we will feel that we are experiencing personal visits with God.

> *Surpassing the peace and joy of experiencing the new earth will be worshipping our dear Lord face to face.*

\*\*\*

In the prime of our being, filled with energy and ambition, what will we do with all of our time on the new earth?

Working at Andrews University's Department of Chemistry, I always looked forward to the beginning of a new school year. It was at the beginning of the fall quarter that we received a brand new bulletin, listing all the course offerings. In the first pages of the bulletin was a list of the faculty committees and their memberships. As we had rotating memberships in these committees, it was here that we found out on which university committees we would serve for the coming year. Each group had a different focus and I found these assignments interesting and enjoyable.

Thinking that life on the new earth may be a little bit like working at a Christian university, it may be that we will be given enjoyable assignments to help us become productive members of the new society.

Beyond that, we will have a lot of learning ahead of us! Naturally, we would want to find out the true history of earth, from Eden to Eden. The leaders and shakers of every phase of earth's history will relate to us what it was like in their times. (It is assumed here that there will be representatives of every age on the new earth.) We have the prospect of interacting with all the prophets, great philosophers, artists, musicians, composers, explorers, writers and scientists of the past.

Suppose we will see composers of the likes of Mozart, Beethoven, Verdi, Vivaldi and J. S. Bach on the new earth! Surely they will be inspired to compose new music to the glory of God! Their works will add to the unnumbered musical pieces composers of the entire universe have already created. Harp music, beautiful as it is, will not be the only instrument used. Orchestras composed of hundreds, if not thousands, of different musical instruments will play the most sublime melodies to the glory of God, accompanied by gigantic choirs of the best voices.

We would also want to know what our own ancestors were doing through earth's history. Perhaps there will be museum-like institutions on the new earth where one could enter his or her old earthly name and other identifying data into a device and out would come a printout containing the names and brief life-synopses of all our genetic ancestors, all the way back to Adam. This way we could find out what our genetic forerunners did with their genes.

Our memories will be such that we will not have to write down anything for fear of forgetting. However, we will need to formulate our thoughts on many subjects and we will need media to capture and communicate them.

In recent years, the varieties of interpersonal communications have reached unimaginable success, primarily by using a variety of computer-based systems and the Internet. Thus, it will not surprise us if we will be able communicate at will with the many millions of our brothers and sisters on the new earth. Interacting at will with our blood relatives (all of humanity!) will heighten our sense of well-being and satisfaction.

\*\*\*

When we look at the night sky away from city lights, we find no words that adequately express our astonishment at the profusion of lights filling our view. Some of the lights may originate from single stars, others could be entire galaxies.

Astronomers tell us about galaxies, black holes, supernovae, the birth and death of stars in the universe. It is remarkable how much information astronomers are able to squeeze out of the various forms of electromagnetic radiations reaching us from outer space. But given that their underlying assumptions about the nature of the universe is suspect, it is also possible that their conclusions also need to be taken with a grain of salt.

Bible believing Christians hold that it is the Creator that brought into existence everything in the cosmos and that He upholds galaxies and star systems in an orderly manner. There does not seem to be any room for colliding galaxies or exploding stars in our version of the universe.

We do not know what to make of quasi-stellar radio sources (quasars), emitters of enormous amounts of visible light and radio waves. Astronomers tell us that there are supermassive black holes surrounded by gaseous disks. Perhaps.

What is certain is that on the earth made new, we will learn of the true identity of every celestial phenomenon. The seemingly mind-boggling complexities of the universe will be made understandable by our Creator. We will learn about the characteristic features of the various regions of the universe. If there are indeed trillions of galaxies, it will take some time to learn the salient features of each! We are talking centuries, if not millennia! Time will not be a limiting factor!

\*\*\*

There were very good reasons for the Creator to bring Homo sapiens, created in the image of the Lord, into a universe already bustling with created beings of the non-human variety. Humans were created in the image of God, not only in appearance but also in temperament and character.[49] With the fall of mankind, this image has almost been lost, but it will be restored on the new earth. There, humans will be suitable representatives of God to the inhabitants of the universe. How the Lord will choose humans to bless the universe is not known. Certainly there will be work for us to do, exciting and noble tasks, which will make God's wonderful universe an even better place!

\*\*\*

Thinking about eternal life on the new earth is a pleasant and positive experience, but we are still here on the old earth and must deal with the challenges that are part and parcels of it. If our attention is mainly on the hereafter, we are in danger of neglecting our present obligations, both in the family and in society. Such practices inevitably cause tensions and/or unhappiness in our surroundings, both in society and at home.

---

[49]Ellen G. White, Patriarchs and Prophets (Washington, DC: Review and Herald, 1890), p. 45.

Fortunately, there is a way to combine our present realities with our hope for the future. The key is a verse in the Bible: "I write these things to you who believe in the name of the Son of God so that you may know that you have eternal life" (1 John 5:13, NIV). Thus, when we look upon the Savior of the world and ask for forgiveness of our sins in His name and by His merits, we not only obtain what we ask for, but we are given eternal life at that very moment! We do not have to wait to be resurrected from the dead or to be caught up in air to meet Jesus if we are alive at His second coming!

Should we die before earth's current history comes to its end, we shall merely sleep until the resurrection. To us, this will feel exactly like when we go to sleep at night and wake up to a brand new morning.

What then should we do with this exciting concept that, while on this old earth, we already have eternal life? We make the concept of eternal life a reality in our own world! For starters, we treat everyone in our sphere of influence—family, friends and even strangers—as if we are living on the new earth already!

In whatever situation we find ourselves, we need to keep in the forefront of our consciousness that we will be citizens of the new earth. Therefore, our words and general behavior should reflect this conviction. Knowing that all bad behavior stems from our bent to selfishness is a great help! It is in our power to examine our motives and interactions with everyone and see to it that they are in harmony with the great law—to love our fellow humans as ourselves!

*In whatever situation we find ourselves, we need to keep in the forefront of our consciousness that we will be citizens of the new earth.*

The joys of the new earth will largely consist of the cordial and loving treatment we will receive from every corner! Radiating unselfish love to everyone in our sphere of influence will be a great tune-up for life eternal on the new earth. As we seek to uplift all with whom we come in contact, our love for our great God will increase forever!

## Appendix 1

# How Radioactivity is Used to Estimate the Age of the Earth

All matter on earth is composed of various combinations of ninety-four different kinds of substances, called elements. Elements cannot be changed in the chemical laboratory to any other substance. Examples of elements are the gases hydrogen and oxygen, the solids of carbon, silver and gold. In addition, there are twenty-four different kinds of synthetic elements that are man-made.

Pure elements are composed of tiny particles called atoms. They are so small that we need very special equipment to visualize them, called an atomic force microscope.

The structure of every atom of an element is identical, a sphere with a tiny nucleus inside. Within the tiny nuclei of atoms are the particles we call protons, which are positively charged, and neutrons, which do not carry any charge. These are the components that provide the actual mass of the atom, because the space inside of the atoms is negatively charged, mostly empty space. The number of protons inside the nuclei are identical to the number of electrons outside the nuclei. This way, atoms have a net zero charge. They are neutral.

# Appendix 1

Every element has a unique, characteristic number of protons. Hydrogen, element number one, contains one proton in its nucleus. Carbon, element number six, has six protons. Gold, element number seventy-nine, has seventy-nine protons. Thus, the number of protons in the nucleus define the element.

There are numerous elements that have different numbers of neutrons in their nuclei. For example, there is a type of hydrogen which carries a proton and two neutrons in its nucleus. This hydrogen is called tritium and it is an isotope of the "regular" hydrogen which does not have any neutrons in its nucleus. Isotopes are variations of an element with differing numbers of neutrons.

Among the ninety-four different elements, there are radioactive isotopes. These are elements with unstable nuclei. That is, their nuclei slowly disintegrate by emitting different types of radiations. One such radioactive isotope is uranium-238. Through a series of radioactive events it disintegrates into lead-206, which is no longer radioactive. The half-life of this series of transformation is 4.47 billion years. That is, if we would start out with a pure sample of uranium-238, one-half of that sample would turn into lead-206 in 4.47 billion years! Thus, scientists measure the ratio of the "mother" element (uranium-238) to the "daughter" element (lead-206) and, knowing the half-life of the conversion time, calculate the age of the sample. It is assumed that at the time of formation of the sample there was no "daughter" material present. But when it comes to Creation, the Bible tells us that everything on earth was in a mature state, having an "apparent" age. Therefore, it is not at all clear that there were no "daughter" substances mixed with the "parent" material at Creation.

# Appendix 2

# Biblical Data on the Age of the Earth

| Event | Date | Elapsed Time | Bible Reference |
|---|---|---|---|
| Beginning of Construction of Solomon's Temple | 965 BC | | 1 Kings 6:1 |
| | | 480 years | |
| Exodus | 1445 BC | | Genesis 14:10 Exodus 12:40 |
| | | 430 years | |
| Abraham Enters Canaan | 1875 BC | | Genesis 12:4 |
| | | 75 years | |
| Abraham is Born | 1950 BC | | |
| | | 290 years | |
| The Flood | 2240 BC | | Genesis 11:11–26 |
| | | 1656 years | |
| Creation | 3896 BC | | Genesis 5:3–32 |

Our time (2019): 2019 + 3896 − 1 (there is no year "zero") = 5914

## Appendix 3

# The Golden Phone
### An Allegorical Tale

The package arrived by UPS. It was quite heavy and it was addressed to the Seventh-day Adventist Church in a midwestern town. The secretary placed it on the pastor's desk and the two of them cut the package open and lifted out what looked like an ornamental, old-fashioned desktop telephone set. It had a shiny, golden appearance, probably gold-coated stainless steel. The dial on top was coated with a golden sheen which covered up the numbers. The handset did not have a cord and it could be lifted off the cradle.

There was a short, typewritten note in the box, which stated: "Direct phone-line to heaven. Cost of call: $10,000/minute."

The pastor lifted the handset to his ear, and said playfully, "Hello." But his smile turned serious when he heard a baritone voice on the other end, "You have reached heaven. This is the operator. May I have your credit card number?"

The pastor quickly put the handset back onto its cradle and said to the secretary, "Someone is talking in here! Wow! What is going on?!"

They picked up the phone to examine it more carefully. Maybe it was an electronic toy with a built-in chip which contained pre-recorded messages. However, they could find nothing. There was no opening for a battery; it was a solid piece of metal in the shape of a phone.

The pastor said, "This could be an elaborate gag." The secretary nodded and the two of them sat in their chairs staring at the shiny object.

Finally she said, "Let's call in the elders and see what they say."

\*\*\*

The pastor called a special meeting for the following evening with the elders. The next evening the elders were impressed with the golden phone also. The head elder said, "There are two possibilities. Either this telephone is a toy or a joke of some sort, or it is truly what the note says, a direct connection to heaven."

The pastor said, "I agree. Let's test it." One of the elders asked, "How?"

Instead of answering, the pastor lifted the cradle to his head. He heard the familiar voice, "You have reached heaven. May I have your credit card number?"

The pastor answered, "Ten thousand dollars a minute is a lot of money. How do I know that I have reached heaven?"

"Test me," said the voice.

"Who is Jesus Christ?" asked the pastor.

"He is the Creator of heaven and earth and the Savior of the world," came back the answer.

The pastor continued, "My name is Milton McBride. I was born on August 12, 1963, in Kettering, Ohio. What is my Social Security Number?"

"Just a minute, please," came the answer. In about 30 seconds the voice on the phone said: "Mr. McBride, your social security number is 465-12-4487."

The pastor said, "Thank you," and hung up the receiver. Then he turned to the elders, "I hope someday I can catch up with my social security number in heaven! I am convinced that this phone lets us talk to heaven. What do you think?"

The elders agreed. One of them asked, "Now where do we go from here?"

Again the pastor said, "This is a wonderful opportunity to get authoritative answers to difficult questions. Just imagine how pleased our fellow church members will be when we give them good answers to problems no one can solve."

"You are forgetting one thing," said an elder, "We don't have the money to call."

"It is true," said the pastor, "but we can start collecting money for a fund for this."

"What shall we call this fund?" asked someone.

The pastor replied, "That is a good question. My suggestion is 'Answers From On High,' but we can work on that later."

"You know," mentioned an elder, "we could ask for the result of the upcoming lottery. This would more than repay our investment!"

"Very clever," said the pastor, "but how would it look if this church would participate in gambling? It would be the wrong witness."

An elder spoke up, "We should ask church members to begin submitting questions to a committee so that when we have the money to call, we would be ready to ask a question or two."

"Excellent point," agreed everyone.

The pastor still had a question about the golden phone. He lifted its receiver one more time. When he heard the now familiar voice on the other end he said, "We are going to collect some funds so that we can use this phone. In the meanwhile, would you mind telling us what you plan to do with the money you get for the calls?"

This was the answer from the phone: "We sponsor a variety of missionary projects with the funds. Last century it was the ingathering program, but since it is a new century and a new millennium, it was decided to use a more revolutionary approach."

"Thank you," said the pastor, and he hung up.

The next Sabbath the pastor addressed the congregation, "Last week the church received a package which turned out to be a golden phone." He showed the golden phone to the congregation.

"A note that came with it said that this is a direct line to heaven. Now you will note that it does not have a cord, yet it is possible to carry out a conversation on it. Moreover, we have checked out the quality of information that we can receive through it and, take my word for it, it is impressive. There is only one barrier to the unlimited use of this phone—money. One minute of conversation costs ten thousand dollars. Naturally, we do not, at this time, have the funds to make a call. But the elders and I propose that we start a fund, called 'Answers From On High' for the future. In addition, we ask the congregation to think of questions that we may want to have answered once we have the money. You may put your questions in the offering plate. Since this is the church's business, we would want to ask questions of heaven, which are of general interest to the church. So, please do not submit questions of personal nature."

In the weeks that followed, questions began arriving in the offering plate and money began trickling into the 'Answers From On High' fund.

Three months later, the pastor gave a sermon entitled, "The $100,000 Sermon."

The pastor began, "Older folks will recall the famous quiz show on television called 'The $64,000 Question.' In this program, contestants could win big sums of money by answering questions in a particular category. As all of you know, this church has been given the chance not to answer, but to ask ten thousand dollar questions. We requested from our church members questions that would be of general interest to the church as a whole. We also opened an account called 'Answers From On High' and we already have two hundred sixty-four dollars and sixty-eight cents in it. At this rate, we will have enough money to ask a question of heaven in nine-and-a-half years."

He continued, "So, because there was no hurry, I put the questions that were coming from the congregation into a large manila envelope, and did not look at them. But last week I became curious as to the kinds of questions my congregation had of heaven, and I began reading them. I wish to share ten questions and I will proceed to give answers from the Bible. I assume that if heaven would answer, it would be the same as the biblical answers. So, if I am correct, I am saving one hundred thousand dollars for the church. Here are the ten questions and their corresponding answers.

1. When will Jesus return? Matthew 24:36, NKJV: "But of that day and hour no one knows, not even the angels of heaven, but My Father only."
2. What should our local church be doing now? 2 Timothy 4:2, NKJV: "Preach the word! Be ready in season *and* out of season. Convince, rebuke, exhort, with all longsuffering and teaching."

3. What must we do to be saved? Acts 16:30–31, NKJV: "And he brought them out and said, "Sirs, what must I do to be saved?" So they said, "Believe on the Lord Jesus Christ, and you will be saved, you and your household.""
4. What specific programs should our local church pursue? Matthew 18:18–19, NKJV: ""Assuredly, I say to you, whatever you bind on earth will be bound in heaven, and whatever you loose on earth will be loosed in heaven. Again I say to you that if two of you agree on earth concerning anything that they ask, it will be done for them by my Father in heaven.""
5. How can we increase our membership? John 13:34, NKJV: "A new commandment I give to you, that you love one another; as I have loved you."
6. How to deal with temptations? 1 Timothy 6:11, NKJV: "But you, O man of God, flee these things and pursue righteousness, godliness, faith, love, patience, gentleness."
7. How to deal with chronic illness? James 5:14–15, KJV: "Is any sick among you? let him call for the elders of the church; and let them pray over him, anointing him with oil in the name of the Lord: And the prayer of faith shall save the sick."
8. Why has Jesus not returned yet? 2 Peter 3:9, NKJV: "The Lord is not slack concerning *His* promise as some count slackness, but is longsuffering toward us, not willing that any should perish but that all should come to repentance."
9. What is our true origin? Genesis 1:27, NKJV: "So God created man in His *own* image; in the image of God He created him; male and female He created them."
10. What is it going to be like on the new earth? 1 Corinthians 2:9, NKJV: ""'Eye has not seen, nor ear heard, nor have entered into the heart of man the things which God has prepared for those who love Him.""

The pastor continued, "I think you will agree with me, that the large majority of questions we may wish to ask heaven appear to have been answered already in the Bible. At ten thousand dollars per answer, the Bible may contain millions of dollars worth of 'Answers From On High.'"

The pastor concluded with these words, "Since we are not in a financial position to actually make calls to heaven, I propose that we place the golden phone in the foyer of the church as a reminder to all of us that heaven communicates with us through the Bible."

In time the golden phone was put away in one of the many closets of the church as it merely gathered dust in the foyer. But our Bibles remain with us to this day, and because of that, heaven is near.

\*\*\*

Esteemed Reader: Your opinions, comments, questions are of great interest to this writer. If you care to share any of these, you can send them to: gjavor@llu.edu.

## Previous Books by the Author

*Once Upon a Molecule*. 1979– Southern Publishing Association, Nashville, Tennessee

*The Challenge of Cancer*. 1980– Southern Publishing Association. Nashville, Tennessee

*Evidences for Creation*. 2005– Review and Herald Publishing Association, Hagerstown, Maryland

*A Scientist Celebrates Creation*. 2012– TEACH Services Inc.

# Bibliography

Berra, T.M. *Evolution and the Myth of Creationism.* Stanford, CA: Standford University Press, 1990.

Cook, Gareth. "Project on the origins of life launched Harvard joining debate on evolution." *Globe Staff,* August 14, 2005.

DeVoe, Howard. *Thermodynamics and Chemistry.* 2$^{nd}$ ed. online version 10, 2020.

"Earl Wilson Quotes." Brainy Quote. https://1ref.us/17z (accessed 5/5/2020).

"Electron." Wikipedia. https://1ref.us/17v (accessed 5/5/2020).

"Ellen G. White." Wikipedia. https://1ref.us/17q (accessed 5/5/2020).

"25 Famous Predictions That Were Completely Wrong." Blaze Press. https://1ref.us/184 (accessed 5/5/2020).

Fountain, Henry. "Two Trillion Galaxies, at the Very Least." *New York Times,* October 17, 2016.

Frater, Jamie. "Top 30 Failed Technology Predictions." ListVerse. https://1ref.us/185 (accessed 5/5/2020).

Godfrey, L.R. *Scientists Confront Creationists.* Toronto: George J. McLeod Limited, 1983.

Hayflick, L. "The limited *in vitro* lifetime of human diploid cell strains." *Experimental Cell Research* 37, no. 3 (March 1965).

Higgins, Chris. "Bad Predictions." Mental Floss. https://1ref.us/186 (accessed 5/5/2020).

Hilton, James. *The Lost Horizon*. New York, NY: William Morrow and Co, 1933.
"History of Writing." Wikipedia. https://1ref.us/17y (accessed 5/5/2020).
Javor, G.T. "A Creationists View of the Solar System." *Dialogue* 27, no. 2 (2005).
Javor, G. T. *A Scientist Celebrates Creation*. Ringold, GA: Teach Services Inc, 2012.
Javor, G.T. "Does a Sin Gene Exist?" *Ministry* 82 (January 2010).
Javor, G. T. "Evolution in the Classroom." *Letters to Microbe Magazine* 3, no. 5 (2008).
Langdon, Stephen. "A BABYLONIAN DREAM TABLET ON THE INTERPRETATION OF DREAMS." Penn Museum. https://1ref.us/187 (accessed 5/5/2020).
"Lee De Forest Quotes." Brainy Quote. https://1ref.us/182 (accessed 5/5/2020).
Martill, D.M., H. Tischlinger, and N.R. Longrich. "A four-legged snake from the Early Cretaceous of Gondwana." *Science,* July 24, 2015.
Miller, S. L. "Production of Amino Acids Under Possible Primitive Earth Conditions." *Science,* May 15, 1953.
Miller, S. L. *The Heritage of Copernicus*. Edited by Jerzy Neyman. Cambridge, MA: MIT Press, 1974.
National Academy of Sciences. *Science and Creationism: A View from the National Academy of Sciences.* 2nd ed. Washington, DC: The National Academies Press, 1999.
Powell, Alvin. "Origin of Life to theorize about universe." The Harvard Gazette. https://1ref.us/17w (accessed 5/5/2020).
"Paul Valery." Goodreads. https://1ref.us/180 (accessed 5/5/2020).
"Search for extraterrestrial intelligence." Wikipedia. https://1ref.us/17r (accessed 5/5/2020).
"Seventh-day Adventist Church." Wikipedia. https://1ref.us/188 (accessed 5/5/2020).
Soffen, G. A., and C. W. Snyder. "The First Viking Mission to Mars." *Science,* August 27, 1976.
St. Augustine of Hyppo: Confessions. Lib 1, 1–2, 2.5, 5: CSEL 33, 1–5.
The Editors of Encyclopaedia Britannica. "Rosh Hashana." Encyclopaedia Britannica. https://1ref.us/17x (accessed 5/5/2020).
The Editors of Encyclopaedia Britannica. "Very Large Array." Encyclopaedia Britannica. https://1ref.us/17s (accessed 5/5/2020).

The Editors of Encyclopaedia Britannica. "William Miller." Encyclopaedia Britannica. https://1ref.us/17x (accessed 5/5/2020).
"Universe." Wikipedia. https://1ref.us/17t (accessed 5/5/2020).
University Of Rochester. "Out Of Pure Light, Physicists Create Particles Of Matter." ScienceDaily. https://1ref.us/17u (accessed 5/5/2020).
White, Ellen G. *Education.* Mountain View, CA: Pacific Press Publishing Association, 1903.
White, Ellen G. *Patriarchs and Prophets.* Mountain View, CA: Pacific Press Publishing Association, 1890.
White, Ellen G. *Selected Messages.* Vol. 1. Washington, DC: Review and Herald Publishing Association, 1958.
White, Ellen G. *Steps to Christ.* Mountain View, CA: Pacific Press Publishing Association, 1892.
White, Ellen G. *Testimonies for the Church.* Vol. 4. Mountain View, CA: Pacific Press Publishing Association, 1881.
White, Ellen G. *Testimonies for the Church.* Vol. 9. Mountain View, CA: Pacific Press Publishing Association, 1909.
White, Ellen G. *The Great Controversy.* Mountain View, CA: Pacific Press Publishing Association, 1911.
"Worst Predictions." Fandom. https://1ref.us/183 (accessed 5/5/2020).
"Yogi Berra." Goodreads. https://1ref.us/181 (accessed 5/5/2020).

## TEACH Services, Inc.
P U B L I S H I N G

We invite you to view the complete
selection of titles we publish at:
**www.TEACHServices.com**

We encourage you to write us
with your thoughts about this,
or any other book we publish at:
**info@TEACHServices.com**

TEACH Services' titles may be purchased in
bulk quantities for educational, fund-raising,
business, or promotional use.
**bulksales@TEACHServices.com**

Finally, if you are interested in seeing
your own book in print, please contact us at:
**publishing@TEACHServices.com**

We are happy to review your manuscript at no charge.

www.ingramcontent.com/pod-product-compliance
Lightning Source LLC
Chambersburg PA
CBHW070558160426
43199CB00014B/2544